POLE FISHING
A Complete Guide

POLE FISHING
A Complete Guide

Mark Wintle and Graham Marsden

THE CROWOOD PRESS

First published in 2008 by
The Crowood Press Ltd
Ramsbury, Marlborough
Wiltshire SN8 2HR

www.crowood.com

British Library Cataloguing-in-Publication Data
A catalogue record for this book is available from the British Library.

ISBN: 978 1 86126 988 1

All photographs by the authors, except where indicated otherwise.
Line-drawings by Keith Field.

Edited and designed by
OutHouse!
Shalbourne, Marlborough
Wiltshire SN8 3QJ

Printed by Craft Print International Ltd, Singapore

CONTENTS

ACKNOWLEDGEMENTS

We would like to thank Magicalia for permission to use some material that previously appeared on the FishingMagic.com website.

Tackle manufacturers Preston Innovations, Korum, Sonu Baits and Shakespeare generously supplied tackle and bait; Preston also arranged for us to use Woodlands View near Droitwich for one of the photographic sessions. The other main session was on North Oxford A.S. water near Oxford on the Thames, and we owe thanks to Julian Humm, the chairman, for allowing us to fish there.

Mark's local tackle dealers – Andy and Martine Browne of Avon Angling; Dave Moody of Reid's Tackle; Simon Barber of Wessex Angling; and Neil Cooke of Bournemouth Fishing Lodge – all provided assistance. Simon Willis kindly entrusted us with the use of his fishing box and pole for some of the shots.

During our research we discussed methods with many top anglers, and we would like to give special thanks to Steve Gardener, Andy Kinder and Giles Cochrane. Joe Langridge of the Sowerbutt's Society helped with research on the history of poles.

Angler's Mail and Andy Browne both kindly gave permission to use photographs; the shot of Ray Mumford is from *Angler's Mail* and the superb endpiece of a kingfisher is one of Andy's. Stu Dexter, editor of *Coarse Fisherman*, supplied some excellent photographs and was also persuaded to provide a sanity check on the manuscript, ensuring that we had missed nothing vital.

Mark would like to thank his wife, Valerie, for her support and encouragement and for reading through each chapter to try to spot any obvious errors. Graham would like to thank grandson Calum for his help with some of the photography.

PREFACE

Look around most small stillwaters these days and you could be forgiven for thinking you had stepped back in time to a medieval jousting tournament. The array of poles stretching across the surface lack only a knight in shining armour at the thick end to clinch the illusion.

Yet it is no illusion that pole fishing has become one of the most popular fishing methods in recent years, and nowhere is it more popular than on those smaller stillwaters usually referred to as 'commercial fisheries'. The method is especially prevalent where matches are fished, but it would be a mistake to assume that poles are the weapon solely of the match angler. In fact, they are now the first choice for most anglers who place more value on almost perfect bait presentation than on fishing at greater distances. The rod and reel combination is not yet dead on the smaller still-waters, but there is no doubt that the pole has whipped it into near submission.

Many anglers fear that pole fishing is not for them, with older anglers especially feeling that they are too long in the tooth to be learning 'all that complicated stuff'. They could not be more wrong! I was almost 50 years of age before I bought my first pole and my only regret is that I did not buy one a long time before that. Now I am teaching my 12-year-old grandson to pole fish and I know that before too long he will be teaching me a few tricks.

Those who are nervous about taking up pole fishing should rest assured that it is no more complicated than any other fishing technique. In fact, one of the most difficult aspects of an-gling faced by beginners is casting, and pole fishing involves none at all. Another thing you have to learn with most other forms of fishing is playing the fish – learning how to tire a fish with a rod, and when to give and take line with a reel. With a pole, there is no reel to learn about. Instead, there is a length of elastic that stretches a long way towards doing the job for you.

There are of course certain skills that need to be acquired when taking up pole fishing, but they are not difficult to learn, and this book aims to point you in the right direction.

Graham Marsden

INTRODUCTION

The tremendous growth in pole fishing in recent years has led to a huge amount of new tackle and methods. The resultant breadth of choice can easily cause confusion. This book aims to explain how to go about pole fishing, covering in detail both beginners' and advanced techniques, so that you will be well equipped to catch all kinds of fish from a variety of waters.

Modern pole fishing is geared to the popular commercial pools, and many fishery owners are developing waters that are 'tailor-made' for pole fishing. Pole fishing can handle sizeable tench,

A double-figure carp landed by Mark shows that pole fishing is more than just catching tiddlers.

bream and chub, as well as carp up to 10lb or more (indeed, anglers have landed carp well over 20lb using a pole, and the biggest was a mind-blowing 52lb 4oz). Anglers are also successfully targeting barbel, grayling and mullet on the pole. It is a versatile method, usable in all sorts of tricky situations for all species of freshwater fish.

Match anglers have for many years recognized the advantages and efficiencies of pole fishing and the technique has become very much associated with match fishing. However, it would be a mistake to think that only a match angler can enjoy the pleasure and advantages that pole fishing can offer. The pole is a very important tool for both everyday pleasure fishing and for catching bigger fish, and this has been amply demonstrated by several well-known big-fish specialist anglers.

More than fifty years ago fishing legend Dick Walker defined the main principles of angling, and these apply as much to pole fishing as to any other type of angling. His five essentials to catching big fish are as relevant today as they were then:

1. Locate the fish.
2. Avoid scaring the fish.
3. Choose the right tackle.
4. Fish at the right time; and
5. Choose the right bait.

You might be asking yourself what Dick Walker knew about pole fishing. Was he not a specimen hunter? And isn't pole fishing all about match fishing? Whatever your views, you cannot escape his principles. They are so vital that adhering to them will have a dramatic effect on your angling success. Throughout this book we will repeatedly revisit his essentials in order to improve your pole fishing.

Successful match anglers have always understood these principles, even if they have done so without realizing it. They understand where they will find the fish in their swim. They take care not to frighten the fish. They select their tackle according to their expected catch, and understand when some fish will feed and others will not. Finally, they choose the right bait and feed it in an intelligent manner.

The limitations of fishing with a pole do not mean that simply fishing a pole at full length, hoping that is where you will find the fish, is good enough. There is much more to it than that and the most expensive pole in the shop will not magically catch the fish!

Inside this Book

The aim of this book is to build up your knowledge in simple steps. If you are new to pole fishing there is much to learn; if you have done some already, you will find that there is always more to discover. Whatever stage you are at, you need to go about pole fishing in a simple yet methodical and logical way. Each chapter will build upon the knowledge gained from the previous ones. By the end of the book you should be ready to tackle anything that can be tackled using a pole.

Detailed information is given on the techniques, the various types of tackle and rigs needed and how to use them, and how to feed the different baits used with each technique. The whys and wherefores of pole fishing are explored – when to use the pole and when not to, its advantages and disadvantages, and how to get the best out of it. The book looks at waters where pole fishing is particularly appropriate, especially the (often man-made) pools commonly known as commercial fisheries, as well as different types of lakes, rivers and canals. There is also advice on which fish are found where and an explanation of their habits, especially their feeding habits.

There is a vast choice of baits that may be used when pole fishing, and these are detailed in full, from bread, worms, casters, maggots, luncheon meat and sweetcorn to designer pellets, as well as groundbaits.

Buying and equipping a pole need not be a complex task, and the book gives information on what type of pole to buy, how much to spend according to your budget and what extras to

For the beginner, pole fishing can appear to require a daunting array of baits and tackle.

consider, as well as explaining how to kit the pole out ready for fishing.

What about all the sundry tackle you might need? From a box to sit on, landing nets, keepnets (a must if you are considering match fishing), floats, weights, lines and hooks to the vast array of extra gadgets – some essential, others less so – you will discover what to buy and how to get good value for your money, whatever your budget.

Fully equipped, the budding pole angler is taken through the first steps in pole fishing on stillwaters. This initial step is all about fishing with a short pole of just 4m; the more complicated unshipping of longer poles follows later. The basics of plumbing the depth, shot-ting a float, feeding a swim and catching fish are covered.

Then the big step to fishing with a long pole and short line is taken, gradually leading you to becoming more advanced in technique. Much of this is about catching small carp, which are found in abundance on 'commercials', but other species such as bream, roach, tench and crucian carp are also covered.

The book then expands on advanced pole techniques on stillwaters, including catching big fish on lakes. Tactics through the seasons, variations on the basic rigs, and the secrets of playing fish on the pole all come under the microscope.

In many respects, river fishing with a pole needs a very different approach, and the techniques required are covered in depth, including trotting with a pole, how to use groundbait in flowing water, hemp and tare fishing, and special techniques and floats for 'holding back' in the flow. Finally, the book moves on to the techniques needed for canal pole fishing, including close-in fishing, far-bank caster fishing and targeting big fish.

Metric and Imperial Measurements

There is a confusion of metric and imperial measures in use in modern UK angling. Many poles are developed in France and Italy, and have been sold in metre lengths for many years. Line is measured in hundredths of a millimetre in diameter, with breaking strains in kilograms

With carefully balanced tackle, big fish can be quickly subdued on the pole: Mark plays a 10lb-plus carp hooked while roach fishing.

and pounds. Pole floats take loadings in grams. Pellets and groundbait are sold in 800g or kilo bags. Yet fishermen persist in talking about swims that are '9ft deep' or hope to catch a '2lb roach' or a '20lb carp'. The confusion worsens with the different generations; those who went to school in the last twenty years know only metric, while older generations may have learnt both metric (in science) and imperial (in maths) and can switch between the two.

This book uses metric wherever possible but reverts to imperial when it is sensible to do so. It does not use impossibly precise equivalents (such as 'a 113g roach' to represent a roach of approximately 4oz, or a hook length '14.85cm long' rather than 6in). Actual depths are never measured even if they have been plumbed accurately, so it is possible to talk of a swim having a depth of 5ft and equate it to 1.5m without confusion.

The metric measures used in the book, and the imperial equivalents, are listed in the table (right). They are approximate because nothing has been measured with rulers or micrometers!

The convention in angling is that fish weights are measured in imperial – for example, a 'pound roach' or a '10lb carp' – so this will be used throughout for indicating the size of fish.

Metric and Imperial Measurements

What to measure	Imperial	Metric
Depths	2ft	0.6m
	3ft	1m
	4ft	1.2m
	5ft	1.5m
	6ft	1.8m
	8ft	2.5m
	10ft	3m
	13ft	4m
Hook lengths	6in	15cm
	8in	20cm
	12in	30cm
	18in	45cm

Note:

Pole lengths are given in metric only (in metres).

Line diameters are given in hundredths of a millimetre.

Float tip diameters are given in millimetres.

1 APPROACHING POLE FISHING

A Short History

Pole Versus Rod and Reel

Pole fishing pre-dates the use of reels and has come a long way in the last 200 years. The earliest pole fishing that compares to modern methods was on the River Lea, where roach anglers used 18ft and 21ft cane poles with fine tips (no elastic in those days!). This was around 1800, when the development of ferrules meant that poles could be taken apart instead of having to consist of a single length of bamboo.

Cane poles were in steep decline by the 1960s: a perfect example of a 1950s Sowerbutts pole.

During the twentieth century the pole steadily lost ground to conventional float-fishing methods with rods and reels. There were a few pole successes – most notably when Kidderminster won the 1964 National Championships catching bleak using short poles – and by 1970 it was a method reserved for catching bleak, and then only when conditions suited it. It was not until the early 1970s that Continental success in the World Championships sparked a revival.

It was a very different story in Continental Europe, where French match anglers discovered that a short length of elastic attached to the end of the pole created a more versatile method. New materials meant longer poles, first in aluminium, then in fibreglass. In the 1960s the Continental match anglers forged ahead, perfecting their techniques along with the use of bloodworm with special groundbaits. Their use of ultra-fine tackle was in contrast to the use of stick and waggler floats, and the long-range techniques developed by Billy Lane, Benny and Kevin Ashurst, and Ivan Marks.

English Methods Best?

In the 1970s many top English match anglers persisted in believing that their methods were superior to those of anglers on the Continent – despite a marked inability to win the World Championships. Various excuses were made: the rules favoured the Continentals, with the limited line lengths, short matches, and groundbait barrages that scared the fish; venues were hand-picked to suit the home team – everything except the fact that the English methods were not good enough. The English anglers did catch up and compete with the rest of the world on equal terms, both in pole techniques and rod

Ivan Marks perfected long-range bream fishing in the late 1960s and early 70s to win a succession of huge matches – the polar opposite of pole fishing. Later, he became a master of pole fishing.

and reel methods, and today the England team is feared, and for good reason. Yet more than thirty years ago many match anglers condemned London angler Ray Mumford for his obsession with pole fishing (although in the same period Geoffrey Bucknall was importing both the tackle and methods with some success). It took many years before their foresight was recognized.

The early 1970s saw the rapid development of fibreglass poles to a length of 8m, but it was the introduction of much longer carbon-fibre poles that really re-ignited pole fishing as it is known today. At first, carbon-fibre poles remained prohibitively expensive, and pole fishing was slow to catch on, but from the mid-1970s onwards it became more popular. Initially, this type of fishing was done mainly on stillwaters but, as poles got longer, anglers started to use them increasingly on rivers, and the popularity of pole fishing continued to grow.

Pole Fishing Finally Takes Off

The idea of putting the elastic neatly inside the pole using a PTFE bush at the tip was a winner. Pole fishing soon dominated canal match fishing and found its place on the rivers. Finally it dictated the very design of modern stillwaters. Canal ace Billy Makin saw the potential of developing purpose-built waters full of small carp, and the rest is history. Commercial fisheries are made-to-measure for pole fishing, and pole-fishing methods have evolved rapidly as a result. Heavy stocking with small carp led to more new developments. Manufacturers designed floats that were better able to withstand the harsh treatment

Against much opposition Ray Mumford championed the cause of pole fishing in the early seventies. (Photo: courtesy of Angler's Mail*)*

meted out to them, along with new barbless hook patterns and better elastics. The French and other Continental anglers had developed poles and elastics for roach and bream – the strongest elastic was only a number 8. New elastics in stronger grades came in as the carp got bigger, and as a result poles got a lot stronger too. The canal-oriented, slim, ultra-light poles of the 1980s gave way to heavier, stronger poles.

The Advantages of Fishing a Pole

Fishing with a pole offers a way of fishing that is precise and sensitive, providing the ultimate in bait presentation. No other method can match it in these terms. It is millimetre perfect when done well, and will show bites that other methods cannot. It can place a bait in spots that are unreachable when using methods. Even the way that it can be used to play fish is very different from using a rod and reel, and fish that are tricky customers to handle can be quickly subdued with pole elastic and good technique.

Those who have never fished with a pole might well ask whether it can do anything that a

The neat idea of putting the elastic inside the pole was a major step forward for pole anglers.

more conventional rod and reel cannot do. After all, you can fish at much greater range when using a rod and reel; it is better suited to trotting a float down the length of a swim, or allowing a big fish to run. And yet it is by facing up to these limitations that it is possible to get the best out of pole fishing. You need to find the fish within pole range, to feed and attract them there. When fishing moving water you need to create a catching zone, which means that it becomes unnecessary to trot long distances. Finally, you need to play big fish using the advantages that a pole can bring in controlling such fish.

This leads to the question of where you want your pole fishing to take you. To answer this you need to understand the reasons behind your aspiration to fish with a pole. Are you looking to enjoy some simple fishing on your local commercial fishery? Perhaps you fancy roach fishing on your local river in summer using hemp and tares. Maybe you fish club matches, or aspire to fish open matches and team events. All of these are valid reasons for wanting to develop your pole-fishing skills. It is equally valid simply to want to try something new. There might be a tricky fishing situation where the pole offers you a way to present a bait to fish where other methods fail.

Different Types of Angler

There are three basic types of angler who might turn to pole-fishing techniques: you may be a non-match angler (commonly but curiously known as a 'pleasure angler'), who hopes to tempt some big fish along the way; you could be a club match angler for whom pole fishing will be more than useful, although not essential; or you may well be a serious match angler who needs to master pole fishing in all its forms in order to increase your versatility.

For the occasional pole user it is a case of looking at the type of fishing to be tackled. This can be divided into a modern version of roach pole fishing (finesse for catching roach and small fish) and a more robust approach that can handle bigger and harder-fighting species (anything from carp to big perch or chub).

Acquiring the gear for this type of fishing need not cost the earth. You do not need an especially long or expensive pole, but you do need to know what sort of pole is best suited to your needs (*see* Chapter 4). You won't need a vast array of accessories to go with your pole either – a couple of top kits with different elastics, a few floats and bits and pieces, and a box that can be levelled will do the trick.

The Occasional Pole Angler

This type of use for the pole is not that far removed from the original 'roach' pole method. The pole enables the delicacy and fine presentation that can be deadly for catching roach, especially using baits such as caster, hemp and tares in the summer, or maggots and bread punch in winter. There is no need to wield the pole at great lengths either; often 6, 7 or 8m are ample, so an 11m pole will do the job. By finding the fish, keeping disturbance to a minimum and patiently building up a swim it is possible to take fine catches of roach. Finesse and skilful feeding make all the difference once you have found the fish. The method can be useful in allowing the bait to be presented with precision in weedy swims on slow-flowing rivers. (For detailed information on hemp fishing, *see* Chapter 9.)

The Occasional Commercial Fishery Angler

Modern commercial fisheries need a more robust approach to pole fishing. There is a good chance of catching hard-fighting carp so you will need to use stronger lines and pole and elastic to match. Again, an 11m pole will do the job adequately, especially as you can pick your swim to suit, but in this case the pole needs to be rated to at least size 14 elastic. (For river roach fishing you would rarely need to go above size 6 elastic.) Fortunately, many modern poles are both light enough to handle for roach fishing and robust enough to handle carp and tench, without breaking the bank or needing the muscles of Arnold Schwarzenegger. The floats,

Modern river pole angling takes pole fishing back to its roots as a deadly and delicate method of catching roach.

Commercial day-ticket fisheries are tailor-made for pole fishing, with easy-to-fish water and level banks.
(Photo: Stu Dexter)

Even at club level, match anglers are keen to win and well equipped for pole fishing: Mark Blake lands a carp in a winter club match.

hooks and lines to match the pole are different from those used by the river roach angler (*see* Chapters 6–8). At this stage in an angler's pole-fishing career the approach is simple. There's no need for lots of accessories, and a couple of tops with different elastics will probably suffice. It is best to make up rigs on the bank according to the prevailing conditions.

The Cunning Seeker of Big Fish

The heavier, stronger approach can be used to great effect on rivers and lakes. Here, the use of a pole to present a bait in difficult spots for big fish is advantageous. Fishing at extreme length should not be necessary. This is just as well, since the nature of the river bank or lakeside may make it difficult to hold a pole easily in comfort – all the more reason that you should not fish the pole at too long a length. As the fishing method is all about sneaking up on the fish, you also need to avoid too much commotion in getting a box into position. The correct procedure is to tackle up quietly well away from the water's edge, sneak

up on the fish, and use a pole pot to feed the swim in a crafty way.

A couple of tops set up with elastic will suffice, although the elastic will need to be much stronger than that used by the occasional pole angler. Rigs such as these are easily made up on the bank.

The Club Match Angler

The typical club match angler fishes a variety of waters, from club lakes, the local river or canal, to (more commonly) the local commercial stillwater fishery. These matches are usually fairly small, anything from a dozen to twenty-five anglers, and the standard of angling can vary considerably. Because the betting or prizes are low, the emphasis is primarily on having a sociable day out. It is true that there are always a few diehards keen to win at all costs, but for most it is enough to make up the numbers and enjoy the sport.

Pole fishing has become a staple method for club match anglers. It can be used on most club-match waters, and with a little thought and

Keen young anglers can find pole fishing a good way to start their angling career.

planning it is possible to become an effective pole angler without spending a fortune. You need to ask yourself some questions: What sort of catches win matches on the waters fished by my club? What fish make up those catches? Are there seasonal variations in the catches? Is the pole the best method to use, or is it a method to use some of the time? Are there situations where anglers are not using a pole where it would be better than the more usual methods?

The answers to these questions can be surprising. The club match angler may find that open matches on the commercial fishery that he fishes are won with weights over a hundred pounds, perhaps much more. Yet thirty or forty pounds wins his club matches. It is clear that there is a huge difference in the standard of angling, and that understanding how to achieve the lower weight is well within the average club angler's capability.

At this level it is not so much the equipment that will make all the difference as gaining a good understanding of how to find and feed the fish. Good bait presentation goes hand in hand with pole fishing and, provided a reasonable competence is achieved through plenty of practice, there is little reason why the average club match angler cannot greatly improve his match results.

It is, however, true that the club match angler needs more sophisticated equipment than the occasional pole angler. A longer pole, perhaps even a second pole or margin pole, will probably be required. More elasticated top sets, more floats, more gadgets – pole rollers, bait stands, purpose-built boxes – are all useful once you get into match fishing. These all contribute to technique, leading to more bites and more fish, but it is none the less vital to find the winning methods. This comes from knowing what the fish are doing, how to catch (and keep on catching) the

There is seemingly no end to the gadgets and devices available for pole fishing. (Photo: Stu Dexter)

better fish, and, finally, learning how to experiment to refine and improve.

There is not much at stake in club matches, apart from the pride that comes from winning, so the amount that you spend on tackle depends more on the depth of your pockets than on any prize money that might be earned. It is not uncommon to see club anglers fishing with a £1000 pole and sitting on a £500 box at a match where the winner will get £30 if he is lucky. A lot of fishing tackle catches more anglers than fish but, if it makes you happy, and you feel more confident with the best tackle that you can afford, that's fine. Just remember that looking good and being good is not necessarily the same thing!

The Serious Match Angler

The difference between the club match angler and the serious match angler is difficult to define. Many club match anglers fish in team events, from inter-club matches to summer or winter leagues, and many will go on to try their hand at the occasional open match or championship. The match angler's fishing has taken a step in the direction of a more professional approach. The standard is higher, he is competing against much better anglers and, certainly if he is involved in team events as well, it is likely that a whole range of new pole-fishing skills will be needed.

Of course, mastering pole fishing for carp on the heavily stocked commercials is only part of the answer. Success on a wide variety of venues will depend on your developing the skills to catch all sorts of species, including eels, bleak and other small fish, in both still and running water. These skills go beyond pole fishing of course, but the versatile and skilled pole angler who knows when and where to pole fish, and when not to, will be a formidable competitor. Mastering these skills takes a lot of knowledge, the right equipment, plenty of practice, and the opportunity to hone the skills with other equally skilled anglers.

Pole fishing takes on new dimensions at the level of serious match fishing. Speed fishing, with anglers trying to catch 200 fish or more per hour, enters the equation. This demands the ability to catch small fish fast, whether it is bleak snatching, rudd catching, gudgeon gathering, or accumulating a lot of dace. A standard pole may no longer fit the bill and the right type of whip (short pole) will be needed. Special floats and rigs are essential, as is lots of practice to develop smoothness of style and speed. At perhaps the opposite extreme, there is the ultra-fine approach – trying to winkle out shy roach, gudgeon and perch in difficult conditions on a cold, clear canal or a winter lake. Fine lines, small hooks and light elastics, coupled with specialist baits such as pinkies, bloodworm and joker, and squatts all play a part in the success or otherwise of the team match angler.

Pole Fishing on Rivers

On the rivers too, a number of specialist pole approaches must be mastered. Pole fishing for eels has probably had its day due to the scarcity of the species, but other methods have evolved, for example, the chopped-worm approach, which can score well for perch and sometimes river tench. Special floats such as the 'lollipop' enable the angler to present a still bait with great accuracy and sensitivity yet modern poles are strong enough to handle big fish. Other river methods are more traditional. Skilful trotting using a pole with maggots and casters is one way to catch river roach and, in the warmer months, this method can be adapted to fish with hemp and tares. The pole feeder is an even more specialist method, combining feeder fishing with using a pole; on

Top-class match anglers show the professionalism achieved at this level.

Pole tackle has advanced in leaps and bounds in recent years. Tackling small and medium-sized carp holds few fears for many anglers, as this 10lb ghost carp held by Graham demonstrates.

the right venues – strong-flowing tidal rivers with roach and bream as the target species – it can be unbeatable. (For more on this, *see* Chapter 9.)

Commercial Fisheries

Increasingly, modern open match fishing occurs on commercial fisheries where carp are the target species. The majority are heavily stocked with carp that can be anything from pasties (the common colloquialism for carp of up to a couple of pounds in weight), through the make-weights of two to five pounds, to a size previously thought beyond tackling on a pole (fish from six or seven pounds to well into double figures). Two other species have a major part to play in this type of match fishing: bream and what are commonly

known as 'F1s'. F1s are usually a specially bred hybrid of crucian carp (a fish that rarely exceeds 3lb) and common carp. (The F1 designation is actually a genetics term for a hybrid between two species and would apply to other hybrids such as roach crossed with bream, but when you hear the term F1s on commercial waters it refers to the crucian carp/common carp hybrid.)

Much of this book will deal with catching carp on the pole, and it is easy to see why they are so common. They are hardy, greedy, and give good sport without being uncatchable. They can become crafty, and the expert match angler needs to stay one step ahead of the carp as well as the competition. There is a constant need to experiment with different baits, feeding tactics and rigs.

Bream offer a different challenge, principally because they are very much shoal fish that like to roam. To do well in a match the angler needs to attract and hold a shoal of bream without losing them to his competitors. The tactics are simpler than catching carp, and landing bream is easier than landing the much harder-fighting carp.

It was the tendency of carp to quickly grow too big to easily handle on pole tackle that led fishery owners to look for a type of fish that would grow more slowly yet remain hardy. Crucian carp are one choice but it seems that the F1 hybrid has found favour. For reasons not entirely understood, it will feed in conditions that are too cold for both carp and crucians. It offers an extra challenge in that it gives incredibly tiny bites, recalling its part-crucian parentage.

For more on the different species, *see* Chapter 2.

Important Factors in Match Fishing

Clearly, the serious match angler needs to master a wide range of pole skills. You may be familiar with short and long pole methods, whip fishing, catching both big and small fish, and the need to understand a wide variety of species and waters, but there are a number of other factors that set the serious match angler apart from the more casual club match angler.

Dedication and Practice

Regardless of conditions, the keen match angler will often be competing several times a week, and when he is not actually competing in a match he is likely to be practising. He will take every opportunity to perfect new rigs, experiment with

The tendency of carp to grow too quickly has led to the popularity of stocking F1 hybrids, which are a cross between carp and crucian carp and do not grow quickly.

Time spent preparing rigs at home is seldom wasted for the keen pole angler. Mark makes up a selection of rigs.

feeding and, most importantly, expand the bait presentation and fish-playing skills that define a match winner. The time to learn new methods, try to develop rigs, experiment with new tackle or learn how to play fish is not during an important match. Although practice conditions are rarely the same as match conditions, it is at least a good time to find out what will not work, without a competition result being at stake. Practice can answer a number of questions: Are there ways to catch the bigger fish? How can the fish be kept feeding longer? How can the bigger fish be landed more quickly? What are the bait requirements for a match on the water? How does the way the water fishes vary with the seasons and weather conditions?

One way to make practice even more focused is by practising with a team. Something approaching match conditions can be created by having several team members fishing adjacent pegs. The effect of different approaches at each peg can be assessed and, most importantly, the team members can learn from each other to refine tactics.

Preparation: Bait, Tackle and the Approach

Preparation is vital for the serious pole angler. This applies especially to his tackle and bait. Gear that is slung together or inadequate, poor-quality bait, a lack of spare pole rigs – all may lead to disaster. As football manager Howard Kendall once said, 'Those who fail to prepare should prepare to fail.' The saying holds just as true in match fishing. The serious match angler may need to put aside one or more evenings a week just to prepare pole rigs, tie hooks, and generally sort out gear, whether it's checking nets and poles, cleaning out tackle boxes, or cleaning and preparing bait; all are vital to success. Pole anglers probably benefit from a well-prepared approach more than anglers in any other branch of the sport. Assembling and testing rigs at home will save valuable time during a match. Many top anglers assemble rigs in pairs so that if they trash one there is an identical spare immediately available.

How do new rigs, floats and methods get developed? This is where the fanatical match angler's constant experimentation to try to gain an edge over his competitors plays its part. Rather than following the crowd, they prefer to embark on a constant search for a winning advantage, or 'finding an edge', as it is known.

Understanding the Waters

The final key to success that sets the serious match angler apart in pole fishing is his understanding of the waters and the fish. Knowing the waters inside out – its depths and contours, and its available species and how they feed in different conditions – means that he can be well prepared in terms of tactics and bait requirements.

2 THE WATERS AND THE FISH

Types of Waters for Pole Fishing

Although much of pole fishing is about the equipment, the rigs, the techniques and the baits, you will be leaving your angling success to chance unless you understand the habits, especially the feeding habits, of the fish you are trying to catch. It is also vital to understand the waters you fish, to know what fish are found in them and how the fish behave according to the conditions. This is the key to success. It is possible to fish with a pole on a wide variety of venues – stillwaters, rivers, drains and canals – but each has different characteristics, holds a wide variety of fish, and requires a different approach when pole fishing.

The pole angler has a special slant on how to go about tackling different waters, because the range at which he can fish is limited by pole length. He must find the fish within pole range, and it is only through an intimate knowledge of the water that he can fully exploit the method. Learning about the waters will help your understanding of pole tackle and bait requirements, the fish present and how to go about catching them.

Managed Stillwaters or Commercial Fisheries

Much pole fishing takes place on managed stillwaters, commonly known as 'commercials'. There is no such place as a typical 'commercial water', and the description 'managed stillwaters' applies equally to club and private stillwaters. This means that everything can be included, from purpose-built waters to managed clay pits, gravel pits, mill lodges and canal top-up reservoirs. Each has its own characteristics, and even two waters in the same category may be very different. Some anglers have no use for them and refer to them by the derogatory term 'muddy carp puddle'; while some waters may deserve that description, there are many more pleasant angling spots to be found among the commercial waters. When new fisheries are developed it takes several years for the grass, shrubs and trees to naturalize the place, but many owners have recognized this and have worked hard to turn barren banks into green and pleasant, wildlife-rich fisheries.

What most of these waters do have in common is that they are compact, with on-site parking. They have good paths around them for wheeling tackle trollies, and extra car parks so that it is easy to get to all of the pegs; this is not always the case with some wilder club waters. The swims or pegs are well defined and they have purpose-built platforms, and numbered permanent pegs, which are a useful reference point. The distance between pegs will vary; many anglers believe that the further apart the pegs the better the fishing, while others argue that if they are too far apart the fish will find the gaps! In general, the pegging is usually close by river pegging standards (often less than 10 yards), but high stocking levels mitigate this.

The main species on modern stillwaters are carp, crucian carp, tench, bream, roach and perch. You may also find other types of carp such as grass carp and koi carp.

Purpose-Built Fisheries

The great advantage of starting with a barren field is that an owner can specifically design a water. One popular plan is to have pools with

This typical commercial venue has several lakes, an on-site tackle shop, level banks, and car parks adjacent to the lakes.

This pool has islands within easy reach of a long pole, giving another margin area.

This narrow section of Todber Manor fisheries' Park Lake (Dorset) resembles a canal.

islands. Being able to fish across to a margin is advantageous, as carp and other fish like the security this affords, especially a margin that is not under the angler's feet. When designing the water, the owner may ensure the islands are reachable by long pole. In the early days, this was left to chance and you had waters that were 20 yards to the islands. In more recent years, lake creators have reduced this to a more manageable 12 yards because fishing a pole at 16m is difficult.

The other advantage in creating a water from scratch is the ability to control the underwater contours of the lake. The ideal depth is 4–6ft, and digging 'dry' makes this a practical proposition. For the pole angler such regularity makes the actual fishing simpler; with a few pre-prepared pole rigs it is possible to be ready to fish very quickly. In addition, if the majority of swims on a water have similar depths, there is no need to have many rigs of different lengths.

'Canals'

A purpose-built 'canal' is easy to dig and ideal for pole fishing. Typically 12–15 yards wide, similar in depth to the lake-type water at 4–6ft, and with pegs on only one bank, it can repre-

sent an economic use of land, providing many pegs in a small area. 'Snake lakes' are much the same except that a series of bends are put into the canal to make best use of the available land.

Dammed Valleys

One simple way of creating a lake – realized many years ago by the likes of Capability Brown – is by damming a stream valley. Examples of this type of water include Longleat and Shearwater, both near Warminster, Wiltshire, and canal top-up reservoirs such as Clattercote or Drayton in the Midlands. The form follows the valley shape, giving an elongated triangle. The narrow end of the lake is usually shallow, with the water increasing in depth towards the dam end. Lakes such as Shearwater can be very deep by the dam, perhaps over 20ft. This type of water may cover a much greater area than the purpose-built waters, and they are therefore often well suited to bream.

Broad Waters

This type of water is usually man-made but has different characteristics from the other types of purpose-built water. Put simply, it is

The dam wall of Shearwater Lake near Warminster falls away sharply, giving a clue to the deep water found close in.

Hightown Lake, a mature gravel pit near Ringwood, Hampshire, offers the chance of big bream, tench, crucians and perch to the experienced pole angler, as well as plenty of small roach and rudd.

much bigger than the canals and pools with islands, giving much more water to attack in front of you. The principal difference from the dammed valley waters is that the depth is far more likely to be even. These waters may be disused gravel pits, although some are custom-built. Examples of this type of water include Gold Valley near Aldershot and some of the original Makin's pools in the Midlands. As in other purpose-built waters, you will probably find a reasonable depth of 4–6ft.

Rivers

It is possible to fish many of Britain's rivers using a pole. In simple terms, it is a case of accepting that the limitations of using a pole are more significant on a river. The flow can vary from negligible to fast. The depth may be such that the fish are beyond pole range, or it may simply be the case that the style of fishing

needed makes pole fishing impractical. Despite these restrictions, most slower-flowing lowland British rivers can be fished successfully with a pole. And even on rivers that are less suited there may be some stretches or swims where the pole is ideal. It works best where the flow is slow to steady, the depth is not too shallow and there are fish that can be caught within pole range without the need to trot a float long distances.

For the pole angler looking to broaden his experience on a river, the slower rivers offer the best starting point. The Nene, Welland, Witham, Warwickshire and Bristol Avons, Thames, Great Ouse, Cam and Dorset Stour are just a few British rivers that are relatively easy to pole fish. More rugged rivers such as the Wye, the Severn, the Yorkshire rivers, and the Trent can all be pole fished, provided you pick your spot with care. This list is but a tiny fraction of British rivers, many of which are tributaries of larger rivers. These smaller rivers can be tackled with success by the experienced pole angler, with the

The steady-flowing Thames near Oxford is ideal for pole fishing.

pole being able to present a bait in all sorts of tight spots.

You should not get the idea that pole fishing is unsuited to rivers. Given proper preparation, the right equipment, careful swim selection and the right frame of mind, it can be a rewarding and successful method, often outfishing conventional methods. For species such as roach, it can be the key to unlocking the door to success. (For more advice on some of the specialized methods that can score on rivers, *see* Chapter 9.) As with any other river fishing, the ability to read the water, understand the currents and find the fish is vital. Get it right and the rewards are tremendous.

The main species for the pole angler on rivers are roach, dace and perch, and sometimes the bigger species such as bream, chub, eels and tench.

Drains

It is not easy to classify drains, although it would be true to say that a drain is a kind of hybrid of canal and river. Most drains are found in the East Anglian Fens, but they may also be found in other flat parts of Britain close to the tidal reaches of rivers. Typically straight and featureless, they are particularly affected by strong winds, which blow unhindered over the flat landscape, and this can make it difficult to judge where the fish can be found. Any feature is likely to be attractive to fish in such a barren waterscape, and learning what to look for is essential. Areas of coloured water, bubbles and surface-topping fish are clues. Mostly the water will be still but sometimes the drain will be drawing off and more closely resemble a river. The species typically found in drains are bream, tench, roach and perch.

Canals

There are two principal types of canal: barge canals and ship canals. There are many examples of barge canals in Britain. Most are 10–15 yards wide and relatively shallow at 3–5ft. This means that the typical barge canal is well suited to pole fishing and that all parts of the canal are

Fenland-type waters such as this one in Somerset present varying challenges to the pole angler; this one is small enough for the far bank to be within reach of a long pole.

Canals, with their regular features, are easily tackled by the pole angler: beware the hazards of cyclists and walkers by keeping the towpath clear of your tackle.

in reach of the pole angler. Ship canals are of entirely different dimensions, with depths to over 20ft and widths to 40 yards, yet the pole can be effective in fishing the near side. Some examples of ship canals are the Exeter, the Gloucester, and the Stainforth and Keadby.

On the smaller canals the nearside and far-side ledges are the key to finding fish, as are any features such as overhanging bushes and rush beds. The much larger ship canals are too big to allow fishing across to the far side so the pole angler must get a good idea of the nearside underwater shelves to find the fish.

Understanding Stillwaters

Whatever the type of water you are going to fish, the more you can find out about it the better. There are several simple steps to unlocking the secrets.

How Deep Is It?

Are there deep parts and shallow parts? One way to determine this is by doing some plumbing of the depth. In each swim, plumb in several places to build up an underwater contour map. You may find that the fishery owner has a good idea of the underwater shape of the water and can help you. This is a valuable shortcut. On the smaller man-made waters this may be an easy exercise as the water is likely to be of even depth. However, bigger lakes created by damming or disused gravel pits are often much less predictable. On bigger fisheries it is a case of getting to know the water through experience and observation. If the water is match fished, take some time out to watch a match and see if you can get a good feel for the characteristics of the fishery. You will start to see how others tackle the venue, see where the better swims are, and get ideas on how to tackle it. Once you have this understanding, you can plan how to fish the water yourself.

Are There Fishing Hotspots?

Do some parts fish better than others? Are some parts good in the summer and others better in the winter?

This is where learning from others and your experience will eventually pay off. Some waters

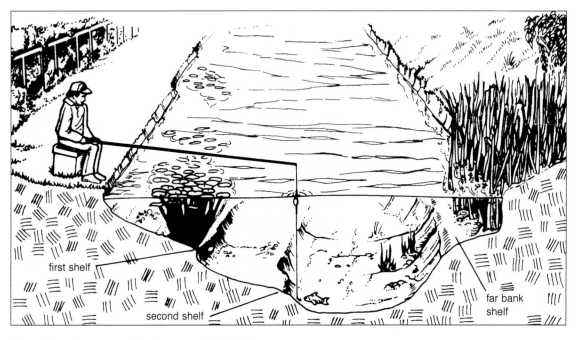

first shelf

second shelf

far bank shelf

A typical underwater profile of a purpose-built stillwater.

have better fishing areas that vary according to the seasons. Shallow swims may be good in summer yet in winter the deeper parts may be more productive. This rule is made to be broken but it is a good starting point and one to test out on the water you are actually fishing.

What About Fish-Holding Features?
Certain features in a fishery will attract fish. The more obvious ones are weedbeds, lily beds, or overhanging trees; the less obvious might include changes in depth and lake-bed composition (gravel, silt, and so on). Where the water alters depth in a step, it is called a shelf. This type of feature is often attractive to bottom-feeding fish such as roach, bream, tench and carp. It may be because the fish instinctively feel more secure when a rising lake bed blocks one flank from at-tack by predators; they are certainly able to feed from a sloping bed more easily that from a flat one, and food tends to wash down a slope to its base. Finding these variations can be vital to catching fish on this type of water. The precision offered by pole fishing means that both accurate

plumbing and accurate fishing are easily achiev-able, enabling you to exploit this type of feature.

The more obvious features, such as weed-beds and overhanging bushes, are always worth considering, but you should be aware that they will not always indicate the best place to fish in the swim.

Water Colour
Water colour is a key factor to angling success. The waters you fish can be anything from the colour of strong tea to gin-clear, and even the same water can vary considerably during the year. The colour itself can be influenced by more than one factor.

The most common reason for water colour is suspended silt. This can come from an influx of rainwater, more usually on a river, but some-times even on a lake. It can come from fish ac-tivity, especially bottom-feeding, which can muddy the water, or it can come from boat traf-fic, especially on canals. If it is caused by fish activity, it often reveals the presence of feeding carp or bream.

In calm conditions, holding 14.5m is manageable; in strong winds you will be forced to fish much shorter.

The other likely reason for water colour is algae – microscopic plant life that stains water a green colour that can vary from pea soup to a subtle tinge. Occasionally the algae will die off, turning the water brown. When this happens there is less oxygen in the water, and the fishing may be poor.

Water colour can help you to catch fish although too little or too much may hinder you. It hides you from the fish and may encourage the fish to feed more confidently. Too much colour may hinder the fish in finding the bait, or, if it is due to suspended silt, it may even sicken the fish. Too little colour can mean that the fish can see the terminal tackle too easily and bites may be hard to attract.

One aspect of winter conditions is that a marked drop in water temperature may cause the colour to drop out of the water. There are two reasons why the colour goes. First, the fish may become much less active; and second, the dissolved natural salts drop out of the solution coating the silt particles that are in suspension.

The silt particles become heavier and sink to the bottom. When the water warms again, the chalk salts coating the silt dissolve, the fish stir the lighter silt back into suspension, and the colour returns. Very clear water can be difficult to pole fish because the pole waving over the fishes' heads can scare them.

Knowing the water colour variations on your waters will help you decide your tactics and enable you to make the best of your fishing.

Wind

Wind can be both a blessing and a curse for the pole angler: if it is too windy, you will struggle even to hold the pole, and yet in summer some breeze can be beneficial in getting the fish to feed. In hot weather, still conditions mean that the water does not get enough oxygen dissolved into it. The fish respond by swimming around listlessly, refusing to feed. A breeze can improve things dramatically. On some commercial fisheries there are oxygenating paddles to improve conditions for the fish during heatwaves.

Water movement caused by wind is much more common. Strong winds blow the surface layer towards the opposite bank, causing what anglers know as surface drift. On a lake, this flow of surface water, no matter how subtle at times, turns over at the opposite bank and an undercurrent (or undertow) starts in the opposite direction to the wind. Both surface drift and undertow can present a challenge to the pole angler, although the pole can be effective in dealing with these currents. Despite the difficulty of holding a pole in windy conditions, these currents are often beneficial to fishing. The water movement often brings the fish on to the feed, and the free bait (loose feed and groundbait) is more likely to attract fish into the peg as its appetising scents and fine particles disperse more widely.

The Fish

Carp

Modern managed fisheries are commonly called 'commercial carp waters', and for good reason. Carp are the fish that have transformed the coarse angling habits of a generation, and it is not difficult to see why. Carp are fast growing, hard-fighting, willing to feed, and tough, and novice and expert alike can catch them.

Carp are the mainstay of sport on many stillwaters.

They will take a wide variety of baits on many methods, and that makes them the ideal fish. Furthermore, heavy stocking can almost guarantee sport in all but the coldest of conditions.

To get some idea of what numbers and size of carp are in your target waters, ask the owners or the fishery managers. Some newly stocked waters have lots of little ones (fish of less than a pound), but most waters have plenty of single-figure fish (in other words, less than ten pounds), which provide the mainstay of sport in this type of water. Many waters now have double-figure fish (fish in the range of ten to twenty pounds) and even twenty-pound-plus fish are possible. It is important to have a good idea of what is in the water as this dictates the angling approach. It is not so much the size of the biggest as the size of the run-of-the-mill fish that matters.

There is a world of difference between the tackle required on a water where the majority of carp are well into double figures, and one where they average barely a pound. It is possible to catch carp of over ten pounds on pole tackle but the method is not recommended for the novice pole angler.

The great thing about carp in heavily stocked waters is that you can find them just about everywhere. Not only can you catch them on the bottom, but you can also catch them in mid-water and on the top. Understanding how they are feeding is the key to success. Carp certainly like cover, so features such as islands, weedbeds and rush beds are favourite spots. Another advantage to carp is that there is no set method for catching them. Simple baits such as worms and bread are just as likely as pellets to catch you some fish.

Crucians, Goldfish and F1s

If you are lucky, you may find a water that holds true crucians. Far from extinct, these shy biting beauties can provide excellent sport to those who know how to go about catching them. Often, the biggest problem in fishing for crucians at a commercial water is that the tactics required to catch them make it difficult to avoid the carp, bream, tench and roach, so that the crucians barely get a look in. Their favourite spots are often very close

(Top to bottom): crucian carp, F1 crucian × carp hybrid, brown goldfish.

in, at the base of the near slope, which can be as little as 4 or 5ft out from the bank.

One habit of crucians, apart from the often tiny bites, is that they rarely seem to feed in the winter unless it is very mild. They do not grow as big as carp by a long way; a two-pounder is a good one and a three-pounder a fish of a lifetime. They are often confused with the feral or wild form of goldfish (usually known as brown goldfish), which have been widely stocked in the mistaken belief that they are crucians. Anglers who are experienced in catching crucians on a regular basis can easily tell them apart, but many less knowledgeable anglers catching goldfish are adamant that they are catching crucians. A close comparison of good photos should help them to realize their mistake.

The brown goldfish is easily the most commonly occurring species, but you will come across the more gaudy and exotic forms from time to time.

The tactics that will catch crucians are usually effective for goldfish. One difference is that goldfish seem more willing to feed in winter, at least on milder days.

The F1 is another similar-looking fish. 'F1' is a scientific term for hybrids of any type ('F' for filial, or son of; '1' for first generation). In this instance, it refers to a deliberately bred hybrid of carp and crucian carp. The thinking is that these fish will not grow as quickly as carp, and therefore

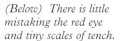

(Left) The small bream is a typical pole angler's target and commonly known as a skimmer.

(Below) There is little mistaking the red eye and tiny scales of tench.

provide consistent sport. Fish for them as you would crucians and you will not go far wrong.

Bream and Tench

You may find that the waters you are fishing hold bream and tench. In general, tench struggle when stocked into small waters that have a very large head of carp, but in bigger gravel pits and old-established lakes, they can do very well. Look to catch them close in, near to features such as weedbeds, and do not fish too light as tench are rated one of the hardest fighters of the coarse fish.

Many stillwaters contain bream. They may be small ones, commonly called 'skimmers', or bigger ones, weighing anything from a couple of pounds to seven and eight pounds or more. While pole fishing is an effective way to catch bream on small waters, on much bigger waters the shoals of bigger fish often patrol out of pole range; this is where feeder tactics are useful. Bream are sluggish fighters compared to carp, and tend to feed as a shoal.

You will find both of these species in canals, drains and rivers, too.

Roach

Once Britain's most popular fish and still held in high regard, the roach is frequently found in

(Right) Roach of this size and above are a worthwhile target for the pole angler.

(Below) Rudd are similar to roach, but more likely to feed near the surface.

the typical commercial fishery. Left alone, it has a tendency to over-breed, resulting in lots of stunted tiddlers. Nevertheless, given careful management, roach can reach specimen size. In practice, this means removing surplus stocks on a regular basis. Those waters whose owners have done this have roach over two pounds, and occasionally over three pounds – fine roach by any standards. Roach fishing requires finesse to get the best out of it, although roach can be sufficiently obliging to allow the novice to catch them.

Roach are good fish for when you are learning, because you can catch them using simple pole methods and baits such as maggots and casters. They can teach you much about presentation and, as you improve in that area, you are more likely to catch bigger ones.

Roach remain one of the commonest species on rivers, drains and canals, and pole fishing is an effective way to catch them. Roach are shoal fish, and where you find one there should be many. It is also common to find several shoals together and, with patience and skill, to tempt the bigger ones to feed.

Perch

Perch are a neglected fish as far as commercial waters are concerned, yet such waters have exactly the right conditions to produce exceptional ones. Teeming with small roach, rudd and other small fry, and with enough features to provide cover, this type of water can offer perch that can reach two or three pounds with ease. What is more, some of the very biggest perch are coming from this type of water, with odd fish exceeding five pounds. It is to the perch's advantage that as a species it is neglected, and that the typical tactics of using baits such as pellets, sweetcorn and meat very rarely tempt it. This means that many

The pole is ideal for tackling perch such as this Dorset Stour fish.

Pole fishing comes into its own in winter, when bites are at a premium.

anglers do not even know that there are perch in their water.

You will more commonly catch perch in rivers, finding them near features such as reed beds, overhanging trees with underwater root systems, and weedbeds.

Other Species

In stillwaters you may encounter rudd, although they will usually only be small ones. Some waters have some real exotics, such as orfe, grass carp, golden tench, even pumpkinseed. On rivers, canals and drains you may more commonly encounter chub, dace, gudgeon, bleak, eels and silver bream, in addition to the species already listed. Each has its own feeding habits and by adapting your tactics you will be able to catch them on the pole.

Understanding Fish Behaviour

Water Temperature

Fish are cold-blooded creatures, so the water temperature affects their metabolism – how much energy they need, how active they are, how much they need to eat, and how quickly they can digest their food. Within normal weather ranges in the UK, the hotter it is the more active the fish become. In summer the fish are more active and eat more; in winter, they are less active and eat less. In the autumn the decreasing temperatures cause a reduction in their appetite; this may be sudden or gradual, and the cooling down may reverse temporarily. The opposite effect is seen in spring, when the rises in temperature lead to an increase in activity in the fish. The blip in fish feeding in spring is owed to spawning, and the fish may cease feeding for several days at this time.

In Britain, the best feeding temperature for most species is when the water temperature is between 60 and 70 degrees Fahrenheit (15 to 20 degrees Celsius). That is a simplification but a good starting point. As the temperature drops below this level, there is a gradual tailing off in activity. As the temperature falls below 50 degrees Fahrenheit (10 degrees Celsius), there are more drastic changes in the feeding habits of the fish. At 40 degrees Fahrenheit, it becomes very hard to tempt fish at all.

In essence, therefore, if the water temperature is below a certain level, fish become inactive and unwilling to feed. The temperature level at which this occurs varies according to species. Some species are more willing than others to keep feeding at low temperatures, and the type of water may alter their behaviour too. Fish that are in moving water have to keep swimming to at least hold station and so increase their metabolism; they may therefore be more willing to feed than fish in stillwater. At low temperatures, species such as carp, tench, crucian carp, barbel and bream are the first to stop feeding, followed by perch, rudd and roach, and finally species such as dace, chub and grayling.

Temperature Layers in Lakes
One curious phenomenon of larger stillwaters is the temperature layering in the water. Put simply, the density of water varies according to temperature and this causes convection currents that can in some instances create layers according to temperature. Water has the peculiar property of becoming denser as it gets colder until it reaches 4 degrees Celsius; then, as it cools further, it gets less dense again. If it is so cold that there is ice on top, and even the warmest water is only 4 degrees, then few species are likely to feed, perhaps roach and perch at best. When temperatures are warmer than this, say around 8–10 degrees, a sudden and severe frost can cause the top layer of the water to cool rapidly, become denser and sink to the bottom. Because the water in the middle layer is still around 7–9 degrees it is warm enough for carp to feed.

In winter conditions, you might expect the fish to feed hard on the bottom, but the water at the bottom is too cold for the carp to be active so instead they feed at mid-depth. This occurs in relatively shallow lakes in still conditions (a strong wind would mix the water up thoroughly), and only when there is a strong cooling effect on water that is already not much warmer than the lowest temperature at which carp feed. This effect is called a thermo layer.

A similar effect known as a thermocline (the metalimnion) occurs in much deeper lakes in summer. It is the area of rapid change in temperature with depth and it only occurs in at least 20ft of water. The water above this depth (the epilimnion) is warm, yet there is much colder water (the hypolimnion) below this depth. Even in windy conditions, the two layers do not mix; it is only in the autumn that there is a mixing of the layers.

3 BAIT FOR POLE FISHING

The effects of temperature, wind and water colour on the feeding habits of fish cause many subtle changes. They will alter the effectiveness of different baits, so it is vital to have some knowledge about which bait to use when and where. There are hundreds of different baits that will catch fish in freshwater, but they can be narrowed down to a dozen dependable types that will do the job well. These are the baits that win matches, consistently catch fish, and are easily obtainable. There are a number of highly specialist baits, for example, wasp grub, but as long as you arm yourself with a selection of what follows you should be able to catch plenty of fish when pole fishing.

The baits have been divided into four sections: traditional baits such as maggots, casters and bread; supermarket baits such as sweetcorn and luncheon meat; specialist baits such as pellets; and groundbaits.

To get the best out of these baits, you need to understand how and when they are effective. Bait preparation is also vital; to quote match fishing legend Ivan Marks, 'Good bait means good bites.' With a little work you can improve most baits to make them more attractive to the fish. It is useful to have a fridge and freezer available to keep your bait in. You can keep maggots and casters for up to a week in a fridge, while baits such as sweetcorn, hemp and tares are easy to keep in a freezer.

Different species, to a great extent, respond to different baits, so you can select one species in favour of another, making your fishing more interesting.

(The advice on pole methods later in the book will also cover each bait as part of the method.)

Traditional Baits

Maggots

Maggots are the least selective of all the baits that freshwater anglers use. Virtually every species of freshwater fish will take them, and that can mean the tiddlers beat the better fish every time. After centuries of use their effectiveness is undiminished, and in the right circumstances they remain unbeatable. The hard part is knowing when to use them and when not to. The river pole angler will find it hard to ignore them but on stillwaters there are many alternatives.

The great advantage of maggots is that it is easy to wean fish on to them. This instant acceptance by the fish gives confidence to the angler that they will work, and go on working.

Sweetcorn, luncheon meat and pellets are better baits than maggots on commercial fisheries for most of the year. It is only in the coldest conditions that maggots consistently outscore them. When the going is tough in the cold, maggots can produce bites when most baits fail. The

A small selection of bait suitable for pole fishing: maggots, casters, sweetcorn and worms.

The most popular colours for maggots: natural, red and bronze.

disadvantage of this is that you will need to fish a small hook – certainly, a smaller hook than the ones you use with pellets – with fine lines to get the best out of them. However, this is a bait that is always worth considering through the winter.

During the summer months maggots can be effective, but on many stillwaters you may get too many unwanted small fish, such as roach and rudd. Many anglers like to fish with double maggot whenever possible, although there are times when single maggot is more effective. Experimentation is the key to success. On rivers, maggots will catch most species, especially roach, dace and perch, throughout the season.

To get the best from maggots it is worth knowing what to look for when buying them. Fresh maggots have a distinctive black feed spot that can be seen just under the skin. After about two days this disappears and the maggots are at their best. Ideally, if fishing on a Sunday you need to buy really fresh maggots on the Friday before. As the maggots mature in these two days they give off a lot of ammonia, so by putting maggots in sawdust or maize meal they will clean themselves. Just before you use them, riddle off the old sawdust or maize meal and dust them with fresh maize meal. The result should be clean maggots at their peak that sink well, having lost their greasiness. Maggots in this condition, kept refrigerated, remain top-class bait for two or three days, and usable good bait for another couple of days. With refrigeration, the maggots will keep for up to a month, but as they age their skins get tougher and they also shrink.

After a month they are tough as old boots and less than half-size; at this stage they are useless as bait. Old, tough maggots that are a week or two old can have their uses. In very cold weather they are less liable to shrink than really fresh ones, and will keep wriggling. For speed fishing for bleak, tough maggots will stay on the hook and last much longer than soft fresh ones.

Two other types of maggot are sometimes useful to the pole angler, especially for fishing canals and also in difficult conditions on other waters. These are pinkies (small lively maggots bred from the greenbottle fly) and squatts (very small maggots that are the larvae of houseflies). Both are useful as feed baits and their main use is for catching small fish in match conditions. Squatts are supplied in red brick dust and this must be kept damp or they will float.

There are two more processes that maggots may undergo: dyeing and flavouring. Red, orange (also known as bronze), yellow and pink are the most common colours. There is no doubt that different colours attract fish, but you should be aware that the dyes are often aniline dyes such as rhodamine (red), auromine (yellow) and chrysoidine (orange), also known as methic orange. These dyes are both toxic and carcinogenic. The maggot breeders feed red and yellow dyes in maggot's food (fish and meat waste), but the orange is skin dyed on the maggots and will come off on your fingers. Some safe dyes are used, but it is difficult to be sure about this. A safer option might be to use flavoured white maggots.

Red maggots are preferred by many anglers.

Cover fresh casters with water to prevent them drying out and turning into floaters.

Casters

Casters, the chrysalis form of maggots, will catch roach, dace, chub, barbel, carp, bream and many other species. The biggest difference between casters and maggots is that it often takes longer to wean fish on to casters during a fishing session. For the pole angler, using casters is a supreme way to catch big roach on still-waters, rivers and canals.

Fresh top-quality casters are a must for roach. Ideally, you should use them within two days of turning and store them in a fridge, taking care to ensure that you store them in thick plastic bags to avoid fridge burn (black and brown marks on the casters). It is OK to use casters older than this for other species, although only chub and barbel seem to relish old stinking casters.

Casters will work all year round but tend to be best in the summer and autumn when the stillwater roach fishing is often at its peak. This is a delicate style of fishing requiring finesse and stealth. Pole fishing is ideal for achieving the sort of presentation that big roach need if you are to fool them. For the angler looking for a change from hauling carp, roach fishing can be just the tonic, assuming there are some good-sized ones present. One enjoyable method is fishing right up in the water for big roach with casters in summer. It is surprising just how big the roach are once you try to catch them. A pint of casters will suffice for this type of fishing. Try using hempseed mixed in 50/50 with your casters. This is particularly beneficial in summer; if you have patience, the better roach will take the

hemp on the hook as well, although you should not be surprised if the carp muscle in.

Casters are a good bait for the patient angler on rivers and canals. Often it is a case of feeding them on one line while fishing another line for two or three hours then switching to the caster line when the better fish have gained confidence. Casters can also be drip-fed in conjunction with other baits; they will attract better fish without any danger of ruining the swim.

Worms

Worm fishing has enjoyed a revival in recent years. There are many types of earthworm found in the UK, and of these three make good baits: redworms, lobworms and dendrabenas. These are all available from tackle shops, or you can collect your own.

For the pole angler one method has brought the use of worms to the fore and that is using chopped worms (cut up with scissors), accurately fed with a bait dropper, to catch carp on still-waters, and perch, tench and bream on rivers, canals and drains.

Bread

Bread is often dismissed by beginners as a difficult bait to use because it falls off the hook easily, yet it is worth persevering. With practice it is easy to keep the bread on the hook, and the results are worth the extra effort.

There are two forms of bread that interest the pole angler: bread flake, which is a pinch of bread

Worms such as these dendrabenas are brilliant for perch but underrated for carp and bream.

gently secured to the hook by nipping it onto the hook shank; and bread punch, which is a pellet of bread that can be hooked on after being 'punched' from a slice of bread using a bread punch. In both cases the bread needs to be reasonably fresh, and a medium-sliced white loaf is ideal. Spare slices should be wrapped in plastic to keep them moist and once the slice you are using dries out you should discard it and get a new one.

Bread can be used on all types of water. It is a deadly bait when fished carefully near to the inside shelf on stillwaters that have crucian carp. Its disadvantage as a bait is that everything else, with the exception of perch, likes it too. Bread is a bait for the more experienced and confident angler as skill is required to put bread flake on the hook in such a way that it will fluff up nicely in the water without falling off. Having said that, the way to learn how to use bread is by using it; once mastered, you will come to realize that it is a brilliant option.

Bread punch offers a neat way to use bread. The punch forms a regular pellet that is easily hooked on. Bread punches come in various sizes, each suited to a hook size, and can be purchased from most tackle shops. Use punched bread in conjunction with groundbait, which can be a mixture of proprietary groundbait, punch crumb and liquidized bread, or try fishing it over pellets.

Hemp and Tares

Hemp is an excellent bait for roach. It has a wider use as an attractant loose feed, or (crushed) as a groundbait additive, for carp on stillwaters, and roach, chub and barbel on rivers. At one time the only way to prepare hemp was to buy it as dry seed from a seed merchant; nowadays, it can be bought ready prepared in tins or jars from the tackle shop. For the hook you need the very best quality giant hemp. There are several ways to put hemp on the hook; the simplest is to insert the bend of the fine wire hook into the split. Only cook the hemp sufficiently to open the split.

Tares, a type of brown pea, are more difficult to cook. Casseroling them is one option, but the

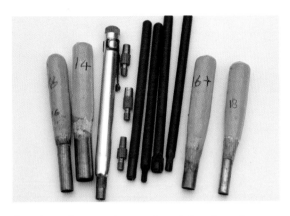

Bread punches come in a variety of sizes, from tiny ones for canal fishing to larger ones for river fishing.

Bloodworm and Joker

Bloodworm (a bright red mosquito larva, around an inch long, that lives in the mud at the bottom of ponds) and joker (the dull red gnat larvae around half an inch long, found in the mud of organically polluted streams) are deadly baits for roach, gudgeon and bream. The pole is ideal for presenting these delicate baits but, unless you are a serious match angler, you are unlikely ever to need them. Although you can collect your own, these are usually sourced through a handful of dealers who get their supplies from Continental Europe.

Off the Supermarket Shelf

Sweetcorn

Sweetcorn is another very convenient bait that catches carp all year round in all but the coldest of conditions. In summer it will defeat the tiddlers, singling out the carp, tench, crucians, bream and better roach. It can be worth carrying some corn, taking your pick from plain tinned (or frozen) corn to special flavoured versions from the tackle shop. You can buy it in a variety of sizes, from mini niblets to large grains, it is cheap, and you can freeze leftovers

easy way is to buy a gallon jar of ready-prepared ones, split them into half-pint bags and freeze them ready for future use. The difficulties in cooking them are, first, that it takes a long time (adding a teaspoon of sodium bicarbonate can help), much longer than hemp and, second, that they achieve the correct consistency for only a short time (like a cooked baked bean) before they turn into an unusable mess.

Tares are also attractive to roach and carp. Fish tares on the hook and feed hemp, or feed tares very sparingly, say three or four at a time.

Hemp (left), tares (right) and maple peas (larger still, not shown) are all effective roach and carp baits.

Sweetcorn is cheap, readily available, easily flavoured or coloured, and re-freezable. Yet it is resistant to tiddlers and highly effective for bigger fish.

with a pole cup. For more on this and other methods of accurate feeding, *see* page 102.

Corn will affect the shotting of your pole float, a grain typically being the equivalent of a No. 10 shot. Use this to your advantage by shotting the float correctly without the bait on, and then ensuring the bait is just resting on the bottom. This anchors the float and registers positive bites. Give it a try, and experiment by making tiny adjustments to the depth.

for later use. Wash the corn before use to remove the sticky syrup. Dyeing it yourself is easy by using food colouring such as cochineal.

Use corn with care – it is all too easy to overfeed the fish because it is so filling. Try working on the basis of feeding no more than three or four grains each time you catch a fish. Sweetcorn is also best introduced very accurately, ideally

Luncheon Meat

Luncheon meat is a favourite bait that catches carp, bream and tench. Anglers have adapted barbel river tactics and used meat for carp simply as a large cube on a sizeable hook (say, a size 8). Use a meat cutter (a tool that consists of a metal box, an internal cutting grid and a means to push a block of meat through it) to slice and dice the meat for feeding. Alternatively, push the meat through a metal bait sieve. The finely diced meat may be fed very effectively, especially using a large pole cup. You can also use a tool similar to a bread punch (available in tackle shops) to punch out a large pellet of meat for the hook.

It is worth noting that using large quantities of meat with this method is detrimental to water quality, so it is best to feed meat in moderation and use it as a hook bait over pellets. Meat works well in the warmer months.

Luncheon meat is a popular bait on summer stillwaters. As well as supermarket brands, flavoured types are available in tackle shops.

Meat punches are distinguished from bread punches by the hole behind the tube.

Specialist Baits

Pellets

For those fishing well-stocked stillwaters, the use of pellets is universal. Even when using other baits such as sweetcorn, maggots, luncheon meat and bread, feed pellets can improve your success.

In the last decade an entire industry has sprung up to cater for the use of pellets as bait. You could be forgiven for thinking that pellets are the only worthwhile bait on commercial fisheries. This is hardly true, but you do ignore them at your peril. Pellets are a cheap, convenient and brilliant bait, and they are here to stay. Originally developed from feed pellets for growing on rainbow trout, they have been used by anglers for at least thirty years, proving attractive to carp, tench and bream.

Pellets come in a range of sizes, from micro (about 1mm) up to about 28mm. The pole angler is interested in those between micro and 6mm, using the 4mm and 6mm sizes as hook bait and the smaller sizes for feeding the swim.

Pellets have a variable oil content; the lighter brown ones are lower in oil than the darker ones. The green ones usually have betaine, a fish appetite stimulant, as an ingredient.

Hooking on Pellets
Pellets are dry and hard when purchased and it is difficult to attach them to the hook. They soften quickly as they absorb water, releasing attractant oils that dimple the surface, and in this softened state they will not stay on a hook. They can be broken down and mixed into a stiff paste, but there are better methods. Clearly, it is not possible simply to hook on a hard, dry pellet when pole fishing. The method used by carp and barbel anglers of drilling and hair-rigging the pellets is feasible, but hair-rigging is better suited to larger pellets from 10mm and upwards, and the pole angler mostly uses pellets in the 4mm and 6mm size for bait.

In the 1990s, thinking anglers developed the bait band – a narrow silicon rubber band like a slim float rubber, which holds the pellet on to the hook. Alternatively, the pellet can be drilled and the band pulled through the hole. This breakthrough revolutionized the use of pellets as hook bait. The disadvantage is that it is fiddly to put the pellet into/on to the band, although there are tools to help. Anglers needed a method of hooking the pellets directly on the hook, and they did not have to wait long.

Bait manufacturers next developed the expander pellet, which is prepared for use either by soaking overnight or by using a vacuum pump to force the air out of the expanded pellet and replace it with water. This results in a spongy pellet. Today it is possible to buy pots or kilo bags of ready-expanded 'hookable' pellets, which come

There is a wide variety of pellets available today, from hard feed pellets, expander pellets, which need preparation, to tubs of soft hook pellets in a variety of flavours.

Attach hard pellets using a bait band.

Soft hooker or expander pellets can be easily hooked. Hook into the round side of the pellet, not the end; they stay on better this way.

in a variety of flavours; favourites include strawberry, monster crab, curry and Scopex. For the beginner these pots of hookable baits are a godsend, and you could do far worse than obtain a couple of pots in the 4mm and 6mm sizes, plus a kilo bag of 3mm feed pellets. If you hook into the rounded side of the pellet rather than the end, they will stay on better.

In choosing the hook bait, you need to ensure that the pellets are sinking rather than floating. You must also check that the water you intend fishing does not have any special rules saying that you may use only their own-brand pellets; if so, you will have to comply.

Other developments include expanded pellets with a flavoured gelatine mix to make a jelly pellet, and a type of 'skinned' pellet ('Skinz'), which is like a tough bag of soft pellet mix. These can easily be hooked on.

How to Use Pellets

These pellets are obviously effective for carp, and then, in no particular order, for tench, crucians, bream and roach. Given mild conditions, you can use them effectively from spring right through to late autumn. During the winter they are less effective, but in mild conditions they can still score at this time of year. Micro-pellets (1mm and 2mm sizes) are a useful winter feed bait and should be used sparingly.

It is during the warmer months that pellets are best. This is the time to use them both as feed and hook bait. The great thing about them is that you do not need huge quantities, and accurate feeding of just a small amount on a regular basis is a good starting point for the novice on this type of water. The emphasis is on regular feeding. This does not mean a huge handful every half an hour but half a dozen pellets every minute.

Small pellets tend to float. To counteract this, fill the bait box containing them with water, then drain immediately. This will soak them enough to sink them without turning them into a mush.

As you gain experience using pellets you can learn when to up the feed rate considerably. A shoal of ravenous carp can soon hoover up a significant quantity of pellets.

Paste

You can make paste from stale bread, mixed with cheese or ground-up trout pellets. The modern pole angler's preference is for proprietary paste mixes, which are proving to be highly effective at catching bigger carp from commercial fisheries. Some are not that different from using a boilie mix – only in that it is much softer. It is certainly worth trying a paste, especially if the water you are fishing has carp that are bigger than a few pounds. Like sweetcorn it is a heavy bait and fished on a big hook. Mix the paste soft enough to be lowered into the water. Expect to rebait on a regular basis as the paste soon dissolves into a cloud of mush. As with sweetcorn, use the weight of the paste bait to set the float correctly, so that when the paste has dissolved the float will rise. As this could also be a bite, strike anyway, and rebait. The paste left in the swim helps attract the fish.

Groundbait

Groundbait serves three vital purposes: it can feed the fish, it can attract the fish, and it can be used as a carrier for other baits such as maggots, casters, bloodworm, and so on.

Pastes may be ready-mixed in tubs or come as a powder that just needs the careful addition of water and mixing.

Pure brown breadcrumb is groundbait at its plainest and will serve all of these purposes. Developments on the Continent, however, over the last twenty or so years, have created a vast range of sophisticated groundbaits with many different purposes and ingredients. Different additives change the activity of the groundbait, from highly active and clouding to inert. Other additives such as crushed hemp attract different species. The fineness of the particles, the colour of the groundbait and the food content of the groundbait can all be varied. It is possible to get hold of specialist groundbaits that do all of these jobs, and some may have specific additives such as PV1 (a dissolving binder), to increase a particular effect. Once you understand the basics it is not that difficult to develop your own mixes to suit the waters you are fishing.

For small fish that are feeding up in the water, you might want a very fine, light-coloured, clouding groundbait with little food content. To attract carp, tench and bream in stillwater, it might be better to use an inert heavy groundbait with coarse particles, possibly with a fishmeal base as attractant. On a difficult canal in winter a fine, dark, inert, low-feed groundbait, possibly mixed with leam, to act as a carrier for joker feed without overfeeding the fish, might be the answer. On a river, a heavy mix, with a dissolving binder, might be the right mix for big roach and bream. Mixes for roach usually include ground hempseed.

If the water has some colour in it, light-coloured mixes are best; in clear water a dark groundbait may be better. The theory behind this is that roach feel vulnerable to predators such as pike when swimming over a bright patch of groundbait in clear water. However, the fish do not always read the rules, and there are times when the brightest feed of all – punch crumb in stark white – can be deadly in the clearest of water.

When blending groundbaits it is best to use a measure so that you can repeat the mix. A bait box will do for this. Thoroughly mix the dry groundbaits before adding water. It is advisable to mix groundbaits of the same type together so that adding the groundbaits enhances the effect rather than cancels it out. In other words, adding a very heavy inert mix to ultra-fine cloud bait achieves little; if you want to lessen the cloudiness or heaviness of a groundbait, a neutral groundbait such as fine brown crumb will help. When you mix groundbait, do it thoroughly, and then allow it to stand for ten minutes as it will take a while to absorb the water properly. You may need to add more water and re-mix it. Many top anglers then riddle it to get rid of any lumps.

For more on the subject of groundbait, *see* Chapters 9 and 10.

There are specialist groundbaits to cover stillwater, river and canal fishing. Fishmeal-based ones are popular for pole fishing for carp and bream.

Additives and Flavours

The pole angler will find all kinds of potential additives useful, from colour dyes to flavours, binders and attractants. Red baits are highly attractive to many fish, and you can also lighten or darken groundbait to suit conditions (light-coloured in coloured water, dark in clear water). With flavours, the simplest starting point is the fact that sweet flavours work best in summer and spicy ones in winter. Use flavours in moderation: a few drops to a pint of maggots or a groundbait mix will be enough. Binders range from 'sticky-mag', for sticking maggots together (Horlicks also works), to PV1 (a type of sugar) for groundbait.

Some additives have other beneficial effects. The Indian spice turmeric gives maggots a yellow colour and a spicy flavour, and it degreases them, so it can be recommended. Molehill soil can be added to heavy groundbait for deep, powerful rivers – it not only bulks out the groundbait, it also gets it down quickly, helps it to break up and, according to some, includes worm essence as a natural attractant!

General Advice

There is a wide range of baits that will all catch fish in the right circumstances. It is probably true that just two or three of the many listed will suffice for your needs but it can be interesting to try out different baits from time to time. Many baits work well in conjunction with another; hemp and caster is just one of the well-known combinations. Furthermore, the fishes' preferences change over time; they wise up to baits, and those anglers willing to find the next killing bait make the big catches.

Quantities

Bait requirements for a day's pole fishing vary enormously. A freezing cold winter canal or still-water might require barely a handful of bait, fed sparingly. A big shoal of dace on a river could

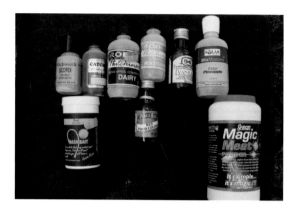

Additives may be flavours or colourants. Use flavours with care; a drop or two is usually sufficient.

take a gallon of maggots plus several kilos of groundbait. A hungry shoal of carp could take several pints of pellets or several tins of sweetcorn. The permutations are endless. What you have to do is look at each situation and try – from experience and knowledge of the water, its fish and the prevailing conditions – to arm yourself with the right bait in the right quantity.

Keeping Bait

Having a fridge and freezer to yourself just for bait has many advantages. Many dedicated anglers have wormeries, and even the means to keep baits such as bloodworm and joker alive for some time. Some baits are well suited to re-freezing without any problems. You can re-freeze hemp and sweetcorn several times as long as they have not been out in hot weather for too long each time. Luncheon meat and cat foods based on meat and fish should be used from the tin on the day of fishing. If you have leftover meat- and fish-based baits, wrap them in a bag and bin them when you get home, rather than re-freezing for another day. Treat meat- and fish-based foodstuffs with caution as they become toxic (with the fat becoming rancid). Similarly, use baits by their use-by date. Store pellets in sealed bags or containers in the dark, and use within twelve months of purchase.

4 BUYING AND EQUIPPING A POLE

Buying a Pole

Buying a pole is a daunting task, but it can be made more straightforward if you have some understanding of the qualities you need to look for. Poles come in different lengths, from as short as 2m ('whips') to as long as 16m, and are available in take-apart and telescopic versions.

Take-Apart Poles

Take-apart poles – carp poles, match poles, all-rounders, margin poles – are the standard workhorses of pole fishing. The most common lengths available are 11m, 12.5/13m, 14.5m and 16m. A look through some tackle catalogues will reveal several types of poles and a wide price range, but what are the differences?

There is a huge range of poles available with prices to suit all pockets. A big show such as 'Go Fishing' is ideal for comparing what is available.

Graham tries out a pole at the 'Go Fishing' show at Birmingham's NEC.

Carp poles are strong, and rated for up to size 20 elastic. They will not be the lightest, or the stiffest, and may weigh 30 or 40 per cent more than an equivalent match pole. Their strength makes them ideal for anglers catching carp up to double figures on commercial fisheries.

Competition or match poles are designed for delicate work – roach fishing or canal fishing with fine lines and small hooks. That means they must be light, stiff and slim. Their top elastic rating is likely to be 10 or 12. Fitting a power top kit to this type of pole makes them top-heavy.

All-round poles are a compromise between the fragile, lightweight match poles and the robust, heavier carp poles. They are stiffer than the carp poles but not as stiff as match poles. To improve their versatility they have both match and power top kits. The very best of this type of pole can do both jobs well, but they are expensive.

Margin poles are designed for fishing close in (in the margins) on commercial fisheries, with

heavy lines and strong hooks, for what are (in pole fishing terms) big carp, in other words, fish of up to twenty pounds. They are made in lengths up to around 11m, although most are 5–8m. They are very robust, not especially stiff, and fairly heavy for the length, although, because they are usually only fished at 7 or 8m, this is not a problem. Margin poles are cheap, usually costing less than £100. Many top match anglers use them in snaggy spots, knowing that their robustness can take rough treatment rather than risking an expensive top-of-range pole.

Virtually all take-apart poles now have put-over joints, where the ferrule of the thinner section (the female) fits 'over' the ferrule of the thicker section (the male). This results in a taper to the ferrule, which makes it easy to take the joints apart. At one time some poles had put-in joints (the thinner section's ferrule fitting inside the ferrule of the thicker section), but these parallel joints often seized. Put-in joints

Typical Pole Lengths and Weights

Type of pole	Typical length and weight
Match pole	11m/650g
	13m/850g
	14.5m/1050g
	16m/1300g
All-round poles	11m/800g
	13m/1000g
	14.5m/1200g
	16m/1500g
Carp poles	11m/900g
	13m/1100g
	14.5m/1300g
	16m/1600g
Margin poles	7m/600g
	8m/700g
	9m/850g
	10m/1000g

are being phased out and a pole with put-over joints is recommended.

Weight and Balance

The weight of a pole (quoted in grams) relates to several factors: the quality of the carbon used, the proportion of resin, the wall strength and the tapers. But the weight of the pole is not the entire story. The balance of the pole is affected by the point at which its weight is acting; a heavier but well-balanced pole will feel lighter in use than one that is lighter but more top-heavy. Manufacturers do not provide an indication of balance so it is very much a case of trying them out.

The pole's balance alters once you elasticate it, so you will need to handle any potential pole purchase fully set up. It is important to do this while sitting on a proper fishing box rather than

standing up. This gives you a true feel of what the pole is like to fish with.

Weight varies considerably from pole to pole. A match pole is much lighter than a carp pole and a margin pole is heavier still. As you spend more money, so weights tend to come down.

Stiffness

Stiffness is allied to weight. A floppy pole is hard work to fish with; in windy conditions you will struggle to control it and find your float gets pulled out of position. When you try to strike, or lift into a fish, it is hard to control the action, leading to missed bites, bumped fish, and frustration. When choosing a pole it pays to go for a slightly heavier but much stiffer pole over a lighter but floppier pole, as the stiffer pole is easier to use.

Strength

Pole elastics are rated from 1 (the finest) to 20 (the thickest and strongest), and manufacturers use a maximum elastic rating in order to rate their poles in terms of strength. The rating is rarely less than 10. Many poles have two types of top kits (the top two or three sections at the thin end), with match kits being rated to, say, 12 or 14, and a power kit being rated to 20. Strength goes beyond elastic rating. Wall strength is vital if you are not to put your elbow through a pole wall on the strike. To gauge wall strength you may gently squeeze the No. 4 and 5 sections (sections are numbered from the tip, with No. 1 being the thinnest) using your thumbs, but do not overdo it.

Length

Beginners to pole fishing are often daunted by the fact that those using poles always seem to be doing so at vast lengths. The secret is to learn by using much shorter poles. Even though your first pole may be 11, 12 or 13m long, there is no reason why you should not learn to use it with just three or four sections (4–5m in pole terms), at least for a couple of sessions. Gaining confidence using the pole at a short length, and slowly increasing the length in easy stages – the next

The carp pole (bottom) is distinctly thicker than the slimmer match pole (top).

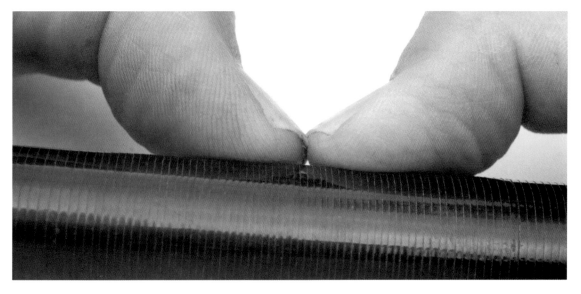

Carefully test the No. 4 or No. 5 joints with your thumbs; they should yield very little under gentle pressure.

stage might be 7m – has many advantages: it is much easier to handle the pole at shorter lengths; and it is easier to learn to feed accurately, to present the bait well and play fish. Finally you will learn that, with a little skill, you can catch fish much closer in than maximum pole range. By gaining confidence and experience in this way it will not be long before you can handle the full length with expertise, yet appreciate using it at shorter lengths.

With extension joints of 1.5m it is possible to extend many poles beyond their standard length. Some poles can be extended beyond 16m, although handling such a pole can prove difficult. As the length increases many design considerations come into play. There is a danger that the pole will droop, becoming unwieldy and heavy. To stop this, the manufacturer must design the pole to maintain rigidity and strength. This is done by using more expensive carbon-fibre cloths and resins, and by altering the construction, taper, thickness and wall strength of the pole.

With poles you get what you pay for – a top-class 16m pole will cost at least £500 – but a tough, usable pole of 11m might well do everything that an improving pole angler could wish for at a fraction of this cost. There is a big difference, in terms of quality and performance, between a pole costing £400 and one costing £2,000, even if their dimensions are identical. Poles from the same range are often made on the same mandrel, but the expensive one will be both much lighter and stiffer, and for a pleasure angler and a top-class match angler who wants the best, that will make a big difference. It means that a gentle lift will set the hook without fear of the pole sagging and bouncing unduly. This sort of pole will also be less tiring to use. The downside is the cost: with the addition of several top kits, the total bill will top £3,000, and you will have to live with the ever-present danger of an extremely expensive breakage.

Generally, poles of 11m cost £100 to £200, poles of 13m from £200 upwards, and poles of 14.5 and 16m from £300 upwards. These prices are a guide only and some long poles are substantially more or less than this, but, as a rule of thumb, for more money you will get a longer and better pole, and more top kits.

What if you do not want to fish at extreme lengths (even 14.5m is a lot longer than most ever want to fish), yet you would like a decent pole that is light to use, well balanced and strong? Some manufacturers have recognized this and have started offering 13m versions of their 16m top-class all-round poles at a much reduced price. For the cost of a cheap 16m pole you can get a first-class 13m pole with all the top kits. While it is generally true that you should buy the longest pole you can afford, you should think hard about the length of the pole with which you want to fish and, indeed, how long a pole you can handle. Not everyone can fish with an ultra-long pole, and physical strength and physique do come into the equation, although there are some remarkably able, flyweight pole anglers who handle long poles with ease – excellent technique is the key to their success.

If possible, do a 'test drive' with a long pole, if you can find one to borrow, to see if you can handle it. You will need some guidance, and to understand what sort of pole you are handling, but the experience will help you discover your own limitations.

Slimness

Holding a very thick pole can be hard work for those with hands of an average size, and one of the advantages of using a pole at less than full length is that it will be slimmer. Some anglers have a preference for slim poles; they are easier to use and catch the wind less but may be more flexible.

Spares

Top Kits

Many poles are supplied with extra sets of the top two or three sections, which can be set up with different strengths of elastic. This is useful, but on a cheap pole you may get only one extra top set. Three is ideal, and it is even better if at

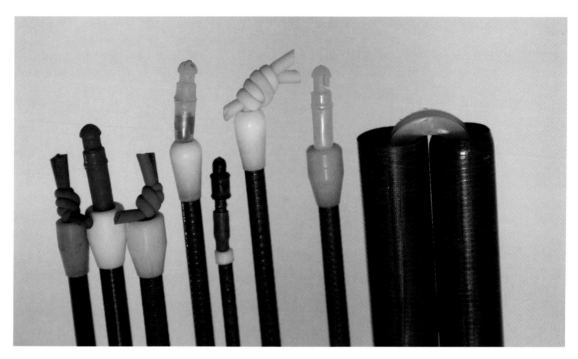

Poles usually come with one or more top kits, possibly including a cupping kit as well. These are some of the top sets that Mark carries. Most of these are set up for catching carp.

least two of them are power tops. Find out how much spare top sets cost. The more expensive the pole, the more expensive the top kits – to the point that the top three kit for an expensive pole can cost nearly as much as a cheap pole. For commercial fisheries, power tops for the heavier grades of elastic are better than match tops unless you intend doing mostly light line work. Some top anglers have as many as eight or ten top kits for their poles. To cover all eventualities in matches they have several top kits with say size 5 elastic, several with size 8, and so on.

Spare top sets and spare joints (*see* above) are available at the time when you buy the pole, and manufacturers try to have spare sections and top kits available for five years from the end of production of a particular model. For this reason, you should be wary of buying a pole that is on sale at a rock-bottom price. You may save some money in the short term but the snag is that spare sections for such a pole may no longer be available when you come to need

them. A 'bargain' pole could prove to be an expensive mistake when you break that seventh section and find that it cannot be replaced.

Sometimes the top two or three sections are telescopic rather than take-apart. This is not an issue if you are putting elastic through only one section but it is a nuisance if you are elasticating two or three sections, so such set-ups are best avoided.

The great thing about power top two kits is that you only need to put the elastic through the top two sections with an external bush, and you will not need to cut the pole tip back. On match top sets, look at the diameter of the tip (No. 1) section. If the end is very fine, you are going to have to cut it back a lot further than a stiffer tip of a wider diameter. To get elastic to work properly it is vital that the tip of the pole is stiff; the thicker the elastic, the more important this is. Another drawback to cutting back a tip a long way is that you are altering the length of the pole; your 13m pole would be 12.4m, whereas

The pole-pot kit can be attached to the end of a cupping pole top with a glued-on adapter (use Araldite) and can be used to feed loose pellets, casters and maggots or balls of groundbait with great precision.

a 13m pole with a wide bore tip would retain its 13m length – it is a big difference.

Special Joints

Apart from the top two/three kits, there are other types of joints available that may be supplied. Extension joints that turn an 11m pole into a 12.5m one are common enough. Special half-length extension joints are for precision work. Many all-round poles also have a special short fast-taper number four or five joint that mean that a pole is used without the existing number four/five. This has the effect of stiffening up the pole.

Look out for 'cupping kits'. These are special extra-strong top kits, sometimes adjustable in length, which are used with a feeding cup to 'cup in' balls of groundbait.

Second-Hand and Old Poles

Check out second-hand poles very carefully, looking for splits, cracks and any wear on the ferrules. The third to fourth joint down where the pole is continually broken down can get badly worn. Again, you may need to replace the sections.

Notwithstanding this cautionary note, there are many poles gathering dust in attics that are in good condition. One of these might make an excellent starter pole, or a second pole for light work. Try asking around the local match circuit to see if someone is willing to part with one of these for a modest price, but do remember that you might get a much better brand-new pole for the same price.

You will not be able to get new top kits or sections for an old pole, so you should not pay more than £100 at most for anything that is more than five years old. You should aim to pay less than one-third of the actual cost (including extra top kits) for poles that are newer than this. The carp pole is a new phenomenon (most date from 2000 onwards), and many older poles were built for No. 8 elastic and less, but you might get a bargain that is a joy to handle and the perfect tool for roach and canal fishing.

Do not touch anything that dates to before 1990, when decent carbon poles started to appear. Avoid sloppy poles, worn, loose or damaged ferrules and anything that seems expensive.

The essentials for fitting a pole top with elastic: a PTFE bush, the bung and a Stonfo.

Find someone who can help you evaluate an old pole and give you expert advice. Is anything known about that model? Was it a genuine 'good-un' or a dire clunker? Remember, too, that poles are repairable – you can get one cracked section fixed on an otherwise perfect pole for about £20.

Elasticating a Pole

Once you have bought your pole, you need to understand why and how to use elastic with it.

Why Use Elastic?

The principles of angling emphasize a need for balanced tackle. With a stiff pole there is very little 'give' to absorb the struggles of the hooked fish; when using a rod and reel, the bend of the rod and the ability to give line to the fish from the reel, if required, help to play out the fish. There is a tiny amount of bend in a pole and little stretch in the line but it is not enough to prevent breakage when playing a fish any bigger than a tiddler.

To play the fish you need to fit a length of special elastic inside the end of the pole. This elastic comes in different strengths known as ratings. The pole elastic acts as a shock absorber to help play the fish so that you can land it. At the end of the pole the elastic emerges through a Teflon collar (PTFE bush), terminating in a plastic link known as a Stonfo (one of several methods of attaching the line). You attach the line, float (with shotting), hook and bait (collectively known as a rig) to the Stonfo using a small loop in the end of the line, and you are ready to fish. The other end of the elastic is anchored inside the pole using a plastic cone (retrievable with a special tool) called a bung. The overall length of the rig is the depth of the swim plus a short length between the end of the float and the end of the pole. By breaking down the pole at the appropriate point you can bring the rig in for rebaiting or landing fish.

Thin elastic with varying diameters, from size 1 (the finest is 0.5mm) upwards to 2.5mm, or size 20, has been used as a shock absorber for pole fishing for more than forty years. Its ability to stretch in a linear manner anything up to ten times its original length absorbs the fight of the fish with devastating efficiency. The elastic stretches a set amount with each increase in loading so that, for instance, No. 10 elastic stretches to double its length with an 8oz load, triple its length with a 1lb load, and quadruple with a pound and a half. Beyond this it is starting to reach its limits and begins to load up significantly so that by five times its length it takes a 3lb load. That sort of loading is a strong pull even with a barbel rod, which has a typical test curve rating of 1¾lb. Clearly, using a pole and

Just a small selection of the elastic available.

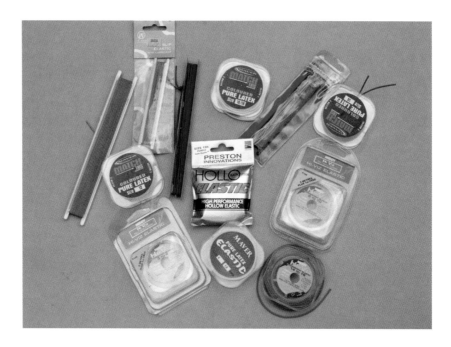

elastic enables you to play a fish with comparable pulling power – and that is only No. 10 elastic; No. 20 can load up much higher!

Types of Elastic

There are four types of elastic available. The most common one is coloured solid elastic, which typically stretches to five times its original length and will do the job for 90 per cent of pole fishing. It is durable and cheap. The colour coding helps identify which elastic you have in a pole tip. Pure latex is similar but slightly stretchier. This is undyed and a cream colour. Many top anglers prefer it, as it plays fish better, but it is less durable than the coloured elastic.

The two other types of elastic available are both hollow. One, Daiwa's Hydrolastic, is filled with a liquid, and is stretchier than solid elastic, stretching to ten times its original length. The liquid inside aids the elastic's recovery. The downside to this elastic is that it is much more expensive than solid elastic and the stretchiness can allow carp to reach snags. It is useful in the stronger grades, and is thicker than solid elastic. You need to use a power top kit and special large Stonfo connectors with this type of elastic.

Other manufacturers have brought out their own hollow elastics similar to Hydrolastic; some are twin-core, while others are simply hollow.

Ratings

Each elastic rating is suited to different line sizes: a size 1 is used with line of 0.06mm/barely 8oz breaking strain, whereas size 20 is used with line of 0.28mm/8lb line. It is the ones in between that you need to understand to get the best out of balanced tackle.

For roach fishing, elastic sizes 4 to 6 will generally do the job. Bigger fish such as bream, perch, crucians, and small carp (to 3lb) are tackled with elastics in the 6 to 8 range. Some winter fishing on commercials, where the carp are not too big and a bit sluggish, and fine tackle is needed (by pole fishing for carp standards), can also be tackled with gear of this strength. For summer carp fishing the starting point is size 10 elastic. This should be uprated if you expect to encounter carp bigger than about 6lb, or fish near snags.

Very fine elastics are rarely used, and only canal anglers trying to get bites with very fine tackle venture below size 3. At the opposite end of the spectrum, the need for very strong elastics of 18 and above should be carefully considered because such strong gear needs a very strong pole. There is even a danger of pulling the bung through the sides of the pole if you get snagged on size 20 elastic and 10lb line! It comes back to balanced tackle again. Strong elastic plus strong line means that the hook needs to be uprated in line with the rest of the tackle; otherwise the hook-hold or even the hook itself will fail.

When fishing on waters that hold carp, err on the strong side with elastic – if the elastic is too fine, the danger is that the elastic will bottom out. At that point there is no stretch left, and it is vital that the hook-length is the weakest link. Broken elastic means retackling, a broken pole, a repair bill.

Use the different sizes of elastic in different lengths. The finest elastic of size 1 to 4 can be used in just a top section, perhaps as little as 18in of elastic. From 4 to 6, it should be used in a cut-back No. 1 and No. 2 section – around 5ft of elastic. For size 8 and above the No. 1 is discarded and the elastic is threaded either through the No. 2 and No. 3 sections or a power top two – in both cases around 8ft of elastic.

Sometimes, having a longer length of light elastic is advantageous, mainly when you are fishing a water that has plenty of carp yet you are roach fishing in winter with fine gear. You cannot prevent the carp taking the bait but, by having latex No. 8 elastic through three sections, you can cope with both the roach and carp – at least, most of the time. This gives you the cushion you need for the smaller fish yet provides insurance when you hook a big one. This is also where a soft white Hydrolastic is ideal. Another method is to double up solid elastic for a foot when you attach it to the bung. If you do this, you will have lost the useful ability to adjust the elastic length but gained a cushion against bottoming out.

Getting the Pole Elasticated

You need to modify each of the top kits for your pole to fit the PTFE bush with the elastic and suitable bungs to attach it to. Ideally, you should persuade the tackle dealer to do this for you. Many will do it free of charge provided you have bought the pole from them, and obviously you will spend more money to get kitted out. Some cheaper poles come ready-elasticated although you need to know what elastic is fitted and how to change it when it becomes worn. Make sure you get a retrieval tool to pull out the bung.

To elasticate the pole yourself, you will need the materials – elastics, bungs, bushes, lubricant, Stonfo connectors (there are different sizes for different sizes of elastic) – and the tools – a very fine hacksaw blade, Stanley knife, pair of scissors, marker pen and diamond-eye threading wire. Take the pole tips to the tackle shop so that you can match up the correct bungs and bushes for your pole.

There are two types of PTFE bush: internal-fitting and external-fitting. The internal ones have a small bore that is only suitable for elastic up to about a size 8; for larger sizes you must use an external-fitting bush.

For lighter elastics, size 6 and below, it is necessary to cut back a match top section. With the heavier elastics (especially size 12 and above), it is necessary either to use a power top section or discard the first section and put the bush on to the second section. If putting it on the second section you do not need to cut it back, but you should look for one that fits snugly. When cutting back the first section (using a very fine-toothed junior hacksaw, or file saw), it is vital to judge this so that the bush fits tightly; always cut less than you first think, and try it. External-fitting bushes can be tested by sliding over the top of the joint to see where it fits. For internal ones it is a case of cutting off just a centimetre at a time and testing the fit. Ensure that you carefully remove any rough carbon edges with a little bit of fine emery paper, including inside the pole tip, before fitting the bush.

Start off with three top sets with sizes 5, 8 and 12 elastic, and ask for advice from your tackle dealer regarding set-up. Initially, get regular coloured elastic rather than pure latex or the special fluid-filled hollow elastic types. With more

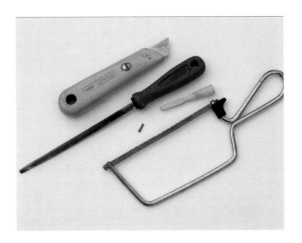

1. To modify the pole tip and fit the elastic, you will need a fine-toothed hacksaw, a Stanley knife, a fine file (for example, an emery board) and a bung retriever.

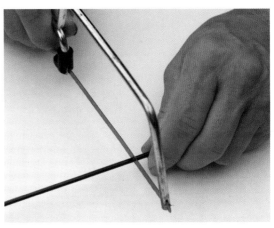

2. Once you have established where to cut, carefully cut the tip using the hacksaw. Try to cut at right-angles to the tip.

3. Carefully file the tip square.

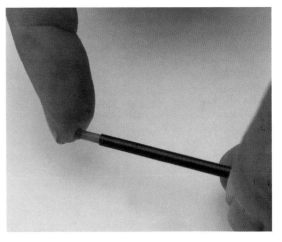

4. Insert the bush (internal fitting) or push the bush on over the tip (external fitting).

experience you may want to switch to these other types, but it is best to keep it simple at first.

Thread the elastic with the diamond-eye wire threader. To one end attach that little gadget called a Stonfo using an overhand knot, suitably lubricated and tightened. Slip the collar over the knot, having tightened it first. It is vital that you do not damage the elastic when attaching it as this is the weakest spot. Get the correct size of Stonfo for the elastic.

5. Push the bush fully home. It should be a tight fit.

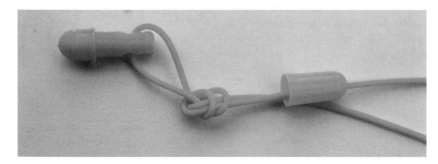

1. Tie a loose overhand knot in the elastic after threading on the Stonfo and collar. Moisten the elastic at the knot.

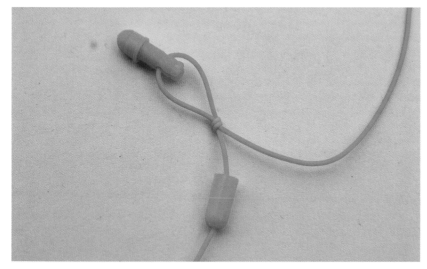

2. Carefully tighten the elastic.

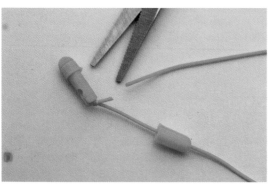

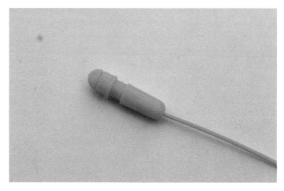

3. Pull on the two ends of the elastic to make the loop close on the Stonfo. Trim the elastic end to 2–3mm.

4. Push on the Stonfo collar.

At the other end, fit the bung (a plastic cone with a small elastic winder) inside the joint (usually two joints down); this is retrievable using a device that hooks into the bung. Check the bung against the end of the joint and mark with the marker pen. Carefully cut the bung using a sharp Stanley knife. You need to cut enough off the bung so that the bung is just inside the bottom of

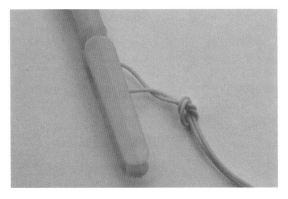
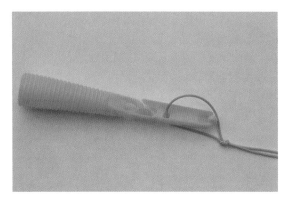
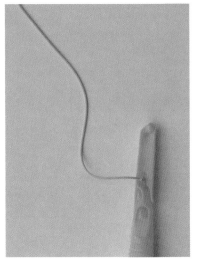
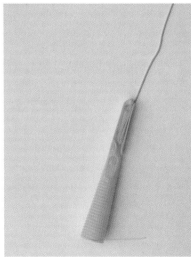

The bung is knotted with an overhand knot such as the Stonfo, which is tightened, and then the spare elastic is wound on the bung. Get the length of elastic right so that no more than about 6in of elastic is wound on the bung.

the joint (about 6in), to avoid fouling the joint that is inserted into it. Check the fitting of the bung inside the joint using the bung retrieval tool. Join the elastic to the bung with another overhand knot, again moistened and tightened carefully.

There are two alternatives to using a Stonfo: one is to knot a short length of fly fishing backing Dacron (30lb BS, not fine braid) to the elastic, and tie a knot in it; the other is to tie a double overhand knot in the end of the elastic and cut the loop off, leaving a 'crow's foot' knot at the end (*see* page 64). To attach the rig, in both cases, form a double loop at the end of the rig. Take hold of the line below the second loop and form another loop. Push this through the second loop and put that over the crow's foot or Dacron knot, gently pulling tight. Gently pull on

the top loop to release it from the crow's foot when you want to remove the rig. The supposed advantage is that the attachment method is lighter in weight than a Stonfo; however, a Stonfo is preferable, since it is foolproof and less fiddly.

Most bungs used today have a small winder, which is used to adjust tension and carry a small amount of spare elastic (about 6in). This allows you to re-tie elastic to the Stonfo should it start to wear at the knot. After doing this once, you should replace the entire elastic the next time. Every time you use the pole, check the elastic for tiny nicks and abrasions, especially at the Stonfo. Always lubricate the elastic with a couple of drops of pole elastic lubricant such as Slip on the elastic at the bush. The tension in the elastic should be such that when the

Some pole lubricants can be sprayed into the end of the pole; others allow you to drip a couple of drops on to the elastic. Work the lubricant into the elastic with your fingers by pulling the elastic out. This makes the elastic water-repellent and less likely to stick.

line pulls on the Stonfo the elastic retracts inside the pole, without leaving any dangling from the tip of the pole. You will find that when you first use the elastic it gets 'stretched' initially, and that you will have to re-tension it slightly.

This is normal. There are times when you need to have the elastic tensioned more tightly, though never so much that it slams back into the tip, usually where you are hooking big fish next to snags.

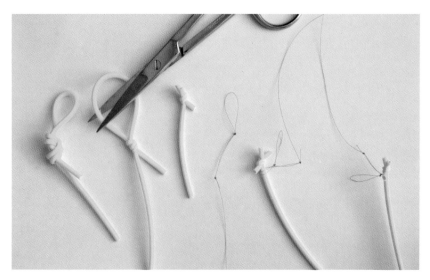

The 'crow's foot' is an alternative to the bung: (left to right) make a loose double overhand knot, moisten and pull tight, cut loop and end to about 4mm, attach rig with double loop end by pulling line through, tighten rig against knot carefully. To free the rig, pull the end loop gently.

Elastic Ratings and Matching Lines

The matching lines are the 'best' fit but it is usually possible to use the sizes either side. For example, size 16 elastic could be used with size 0.16 to 0.20mm line without the rig being unduly unbalanced.

For Hydrolastic, which has a spread rating (for example, 6–10), use the Hollow ratings within the range.

Elastic (Solid)	Main line (mm)	Hook link (mm)
1 and 2	0.07–0.08	0.05–0.07
3	0.08–0.10	0.07–0.09
4	0.10–0.12	0.08–0.11
5	0.12	0.10–0.11
6	0.12–0.14	0.10–0.13
8	0.14	0.12–0.13
10	0.14–0.16	0.13–0.15
12	0.16	0.14–0.15
14	0.16–0.18	0.15–0.17
16	0.18	0.16–0.17
18	0.20–0.22	0.18–0.21
20+	0.22–0.25	0.20–0.24

Elastic (Hollow)	Main line (mm)	Hook link (mm)
6	0.10–0.14	0.08–0.13
8	0.12–0.16	0.10–0.15
10	0.12–0.18	0.10–0.15
12	0.14–0.20	0.12–0.17
14	0.16–0.20	0.14–0.19
16	0.18–0.22	0.16–0.21
18	0.20–0.24	0.18–0.23
20	0.20–0.26	0.18–0.24

Guidance on Pole Elastic

This is only a rough guide, bearing in mind that the size of hook that can be used must also be balanced with the elastic. There is no point using strong elastic with a small fine wire 22. Indeed, for really fine fishing you need to drop down to very light elastics; size 3 or 4 can be useful for light roach fishing.

The following guidelines apply:

- Elastic grade 5–6 is ideal for big roach, average bream.
- Elastic grade 8–10 is ideal for small carp up to 4–5lb, average tench, big perch.
- Elastic grade 12–14 is ideal for carp to about 8–10lb in open water.
- Elastic grade 16–20 is ideal for carp to double figures in hook and hold situations.

Whips

A whip is a type of pole that is by definition 'whippy'. Its flexible action makes it ideal for catching small fish quickly. Its fine tip acts as a shock absorber (in place of the elastic usually fitted inside a pole tip). Whips are mostly telescopic up to a length of 4m; beyond this they are a mix of telescopic (top 4m) and take-apart. These longer whips, which are commonly 6–8m, are known as system whips. Short fibreglass whips can be bought very cheaply, and can be ideal for teaching a child to fish. Quality carbon-fibre whips for match fishing cost around £40 to £60. Top-class system whips can cost £300 or more, although you will not be spoilt for choice. Daiwa have dominated the system whip market for many years.

Unless you are going to be doing a lot of match fishing it is unlikely that you will find much need for a whip, although it can be a fun way to fish. In recent years some 'super-strength' whips have appeared; these have a hollow tip rather than the usual solid carbon-fibre one, and can be elasticated. Whether such a pole offers any advantage over more traditional poles is debatable, and if you are considering a

Skid bungs fit the end of the pole to prevent the end getting chipped. The green one is adjustable.

Steam ferrule sleeves on to regularly unshipped male joints, between sections three and four, for example, to prevent wear. Use one that is a close fit to start with.

whip as a first pole purchase you would be better off sticking to a conventional type.

Other Add-Ons

There are two ways to protect your pole when in use: pole end protectors stop the end of the pole getting damaged when you slide it back; joint protector sleeves fit over the end of ferrules and are steamed into place to protect those ferrules that are unshipped from wear.

A further refinement for the serious pole angler is to paint the top three sections with a light grey matt paint, to cover the jet black of the carbon fibre. This works on the same principle as camouflage grey on the underside of fighter planes. In clear water the fish are less likely to see the pole if it blends in with the sky.

5 OTHER POLE GEAR

Once you have a pole with the elastic fitted, you can start to consider the essential equipment needed to complete the kit. Experienced pole anglers often seem to be surrounded by mountains of complex paraphernalia, but how much of that gear is essential? This chapter will give you advice on everything, from what to sit on, through the different types of nets, floats, weights, hooks and line, to all the other gadgets.

A Box to Sit on

One difference with pole fishing is that, with few exceptions, it is a method that is best performed sitting down. The way that you sit is important – when your feet are level, your thighs are level, and your back is straight, you will be comfortable and easily able to handle the pole, even at full length. There are times when you can stand to fish a pole but fishing with more than about 7m is much easier if you can sit upright on a stable platform. Roving chairs are not suitable for pole fishing because you are too low to the ground.

The most popular seat for pole fishing is a Continental-type seat, as they have come to be known, with a built-in cushion and drawers, and the means to level it through the use of adjustable legs. Being purpose-built for pole fishing, they have trays that slide out so that pole winders and other bits and bobs are available to the angler without having to get up when fishing. Furthermore, the modular design of the latest boxes allows the angler to switch drawers and trays. It is easy to get well organized.

Experienced match anglers have this economy of movement down to a fine art, with bait, spare hooks, nets, spare pole tops (often tackled up with alternate rigs) all to hand. When they catch a fish they unhook it in the landing net, eliminating the need for an unhooking mat, before slipping it into the handily placed keepnet. Unhooking in the landing net is also a good idea when match fishing: if the fish should wriggle out of your hands, it is less likely to end up back in the lake rather than in your keepnet!

Continental-type boxes have been around in Britain for over thirty years, but they really took off in about 1990, when British manufacturers got their act together. Boxes such as the AS1 and Boss took the match-fishing scene by storm. The addition of adjustable legs made all the difference, and this add-on quickly gained popularity due to the Octoplus kits bolted to Shakespeare boxes by the thousand. Suddenly, the dedicated pole angler had the perfect fishing station. In addition, platforms made of aluminium alloy meant that the pole angler could get support for his feet. The drawback to these boxes at the time was two-fold: the cost (at around £400), and their heavy weight. More recently, huge competition means that lightweight versions to suit all pockets have become available.

The most recent development has been the addition of foot plates attached to the boxes, which encourages the perfect pole-fishing position, with thighs parallel to the ground. For the serious pole angler this type of box is a must-have. Add the numerous attachments, such as special pole rests, spray bars, bait waiters, and the means to attach keepnets, brollies and pole rests, and you have the complete angling station. Many are still heavy and you will need either to get a kit to add wheels or acquire a good tackle trolley.

The amount you spend is down to the depth of your pockets. The second-hand route is a

Modern purpose-built boxes are perfect for pole fishing. The foot plate and high adjustability make for comfortable fishing, and combine with the convenience of spare equipment being readily available from the drawers and the many add-ons fitted to the legs.

possibility, or, for the casual pole angler on a budget, a much cheaper option is to buy a plastic Shakespeare box or similar and fit an Octoplus leg set to it. This gives you the means to get the height of the box right, although on sloping banks it would be better to have a foot plate.

Nets

Landing Nets

Regardless of what water you fish you are going to need a landing net. One of the recent benefits of the popularity of commercial carp waters is that the ideal landing net has evolved. These are known as spoon nets, and one in a 24in or 26in size is easily man enough for carp to double figures. Do not bother with nets less than 20in diameter under any circumstances; at the other end of the scale, there is no need for a 36in or 42in carp net on the average commercial fishery. Some of the latest nets have rubberized mesh that helps when netting fish with the 'quick scoop' method, but the normal pan-type nets with a micromesh base and minnow mesh sides are a practical compromise for general pole fishing.

Make sure that the net you buy has the Angling Foundation fish-friendly symbol. You

It is possible to pole fish with a plastic seat box, using Octoplus legs to raise the height of the box, and a platform with a foot plate. The pole roost on the right is there to hold spare top sets.

will also need a strong landing net pole. The best of these are the take-apart carbon-fibre versions, although an alloy or fibreglass one will suffice.

Keepnets

Unless you are going to fish matches you will not need a keepnet. Most commercial fisheries insist that to fish matches on this type of water you must have two keepnets – one for carp, and one for other fish, usually described as 'silver fish'. Again, make sure that they have the fish-friendly symbol. The keepnets you buy should be a minimum of 3m, with dimensions of 50cm × 40cm. There are legal nets that are smaller than this but why compromise when fish wel-

fare is at stake? One match angler's saying applies to all anglers: 'Look after the fish, and the fish will look after you.'

A few fisheries insist on the use of an unhooking mat, a soft, padded mat that you lay the fish on to unhook it. The alternative, which we should avoid at all costs, is to lay the fish on a wooden platform, gravel or even a paving slab, all of which are frequently used on commercial fisheries to make comfortable pegs. Most match anglers, however, manage well enough without the mat, following instead the routine of unhooking the fish in the landing net. A cheap unhooking mat will not break the bank and must be considered if you are getting double-figure carp.

Floats

Types

There are many different float patterns for pole fishing; for more information on suitable types for specific methods, *see* Chapters 7–10. One facet of pole floats is that their weight load is often much less than what you would need for regular float fishing in similar conditions. For example, whereas you might use a waggler float taking 2AAA shot, the same would be covered with a pole float taking about a quarter of that, say, 0.40g. For the run-of-the-mill shallow stillwaters with depths to 6ft it is rare to need a float taking more than about 0.75g except in adverse conditions. If fishing much deeper water or rivers, you will need floats that take from 1g upwards.

Pole floats mostly have balsa-wood bodies, with some made of expanded foam. Many have a body shape like an elongated rugby ball and these are the most versatile. Others are more pear-shaped; those with the thick part uppermost (body up) are best for rivers, while those with the thin end uppermost (body down) are best for stillwaters. Bodied floats are stable and able to cope with most conditions. In calm conditions, a slimmer float is more sensitive and less resistant to the strike. A type of float known as a dibber – a short length of peacock quill with a short stem – is also useful, especially for fishing very shallow.

There is a wide variety of landing nets available today: pan-type ones are usually best for pole fishing, and you should get one big enough for your expected catch.

Pole floats come in a wide variety of shapes and sizes, from tiny ones for canal fishing, to special ones for stillwater, and big ones to beat strong flows on rivers.

Materials

What does vary considerably are the tip and stem materials. The stem below the body is usually carbon fibre or stainless-steel wire. Many pole anglers prefer the tough carbon-stemmed ones although wire can be more stable. Fibreglass is also used. Longer stems mean more stable floats, although the weight of the wire reduces the shot load. Floats for on-the-drop fishing have shorter carbon-fibre stems.

Tip materials vary from wire (which is suitable for dedicated bloodworm anglers looking for the tiniest bites, as it is so thin), through to nylon, fibreglass, plastic and cane. A few models have a balsa tip (the thickest of all).

Float Tips

There are three essential things that you need to know about float tips, regardless of material:

1. Can you see it? In different light conditions different colours may help: black is often best against a white sky; yellow may be better against green reflections; red and orange are the most versatile since they can be seen in most circumstances. Some floats allow you to change tips, which is handy, or you can temporarily blacken the tip with a waterproof marker. Drennan market coloured tube to extend the tip. Translucent fibre tips can show up particularly well. You may need to use a thicker tip than you would like just to be able to see it in bad light or rippled water.

2. Is the tip sufficiently buoyant to hold up in the conditions, and to support the weight of the bait? Heavy baits such as sweetcorn are the equivalent of a dust shot so take this into account. In windy conditions ensure that drag on the float does not pull it under. Small

baits allow you to use much finer bristles. For paste baits you will need a float with a special long bristle.

3. The tip material has no effect on its residual buoyancy, which is affected only by the volume of water that remains to be displaced. If you disagree with that statement you will have to prove Archimedes wrong. As far as this is concerned what is worth knowing is that if you double the thickness of the float tip then you quadruple its buoyancy. This is why ultra-thin wire float tips are so difficult to shot up yet nylon ones that look only slightly thicker are manageable. Although the nylon one is only half as thick again as the wire it is twice

as buoyant. Fortunately most of the pole floats we use today have tips a little thicker in the range 0.5 mm to 3mm and shotting them just right is easy to accomplish.

Choices

Try to avoid the lazy habit of having a favourite pole float that works but is not best suited to the conditions and style of fishing. In doing so you are sacrificing one of the great advantages of pole fishing. Pole floats are the means to tremendous sensitivity in bite detection. To achieve this use the float with as fine a bristle as possible, which nonetheless matches the conditions. Take into account the distance fished, the weight of

Pole floats are made from a wide variety of materials: wire, carbon, fibreglass and cane stems, and wire, nylon, fibre, cane and balsa tips, with balsa, styrene and papyrus bodies.

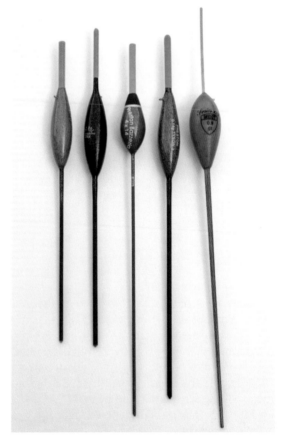

These strong floats have tough stems to avoid breakage when margin fishing or in other demanding situations.

Stillwater floats typically have long, fine stems of carbon or wire. The special paste float (fourth from the left) has an extra-long thick bristle. Shorter floats are more useful for fishing in shallow water or at mid-depth.

the bait, the ability to see it and weather conditions. Before using a rig or float, consider whether it is the best for the job, or whether a different float would do the job much better. If the latter is the case, change it!

Most pole floats suit general pole work with light lines, but for margin fishing and other times when you expect to hook big carp near snags you will need stronger floats. Otherwise you will quickly find your delicate float gets the side eye ripped out, the float is snapped or the stem bent. Some pole floats are made to stand up to this

type of treatment – the side eyes are fixed to the bristle and the stems are much thicker than normal. They may be cruder versions of the other floats, and you will sacrifice some of the sensitivity, but at least you will not have to replace the float every time you hook a carp.

Floats for Stillwater
To tackle shallow stillwaters – up to 6ft deep, say – you should be looking at a selection of floats taking from 0.2g to 0.75g. Body-down types are the most stable and a number of these,

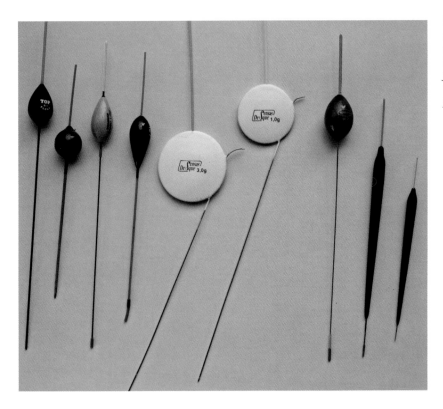

River pole floats are characterized by their inverted pear-shaped bodies. The disc-type floats, known as 'lollipops', are useful for presenting a still bait.

with some slimmer ones with elongated bodies, will represent a good starting point. A dibber or two (only an inch or two long) for fishing shallow or in the margins will also be useful. These will have a very small shotting capacity of the equivalent of a couple of No. 8 shot or less. Much deeper lakes need floats taking from 0.5g up to as much as 2g, as well as the smaller ones.

Floats for Rivers

The starting point for river pole fishing is a selection of body-up floats taking from 0.5g to 2g. If the rivers you fish are deep and powerful, or you suspect that you will be trying to get through tiddlers like bleak, consider some that take up to 5g. Treat slow rivers much like stillwaters – the same float selection will suffice. Specialist pole floats such as the Sensas lollipop floats and Cralusso flat floats are for presenting a still bait in faster, deeper water; they are worth a look once you have mastered the basics of river pole fishing. Hemp fishing needs more finesse

and the experts tend to favour slim floats with modest shot loads in the range 0.4g to 0.75g.

Floats for Drains

Drains can vary from barely 2ft deep to more than 15ft, and you need to match the float to the conditions. Flows are usually negligible so similar floats to those needed for stillwaters ought to do the trick.

Floats for Canals

Deep ship canals need similar floats to those for deep stillwaters; wire stems and fine bristles, and a shot load of 0.75g to 2g will fit the bill. Shallower barge canals need much smaller floats with fine bristles and short stems that take from as little as two No. 10 shot. For bigger baits and laying on with caster, dibber-style floats are useful. Tackle intermediate canals, like parts of the Grand Union, for example, with slightly larger floats, although even here the floats only need carry a shot load around 0.3g to 0.5g.

Float Rubbers

Get a selection of fine silicone tubing and cut quarter-inch lengths as float rubbers. Carefully match the diameters to the float stems, allowing for threading the line through as well. Small floats need two rubbers; those with longer stems need three.

Line

You will need several spools of line for making rigs and for tying your hook links. While a spool of cheap reel line will do the job, it is worth understanding the qualities of pole rig lines.

There are three main types of monofilament lines that are suitable for pole fishing: regular lines, co-polymers and fluorocarbons. On the line spool there are three pieces of information: how much line, the diameter in hundredths of a millimetre and the breaking strain in kilograms. The regular lines tend to be tough, slightly wiry and thick for the breaking strain and suited as reel lines. Co-polymers are softer, limper and thin for the breaking strain. Unlike reel lines, which have understated breaking strains, co-polymer breaking strains tend to be overstated. Fluorocarbon

Canal floats are characterized by their small proportions and delicate fine stems and tips. The dumpy float is a dibber for laying on near the far bank.

It is vital to have a good selection of fine silicone and plastic tubing to form float rubbers for your floats.

Co-polymer lines are ideal for pole fishing.

lines offer the advantage of being much harder to see in the water (their refractive index is similar to that of water), but they are stiffer, weaker and trickier to knot than regular nylon. The use of fluorocarbon has yet to really catch on for pole fishing, although some pole anglers are certainly using it, and it can make the difference in very clear water.

Because the pole elastic acts as a shock absorber when pole fishing, there is less need for stretch in the line itself. Furthermore, unlike reel lines, pole rigs get much less abrasion. As a result, you can use a line that is one of the modern co-polymers with reduced stretch and reduced diameter in all but the most demanding of fishing situations.

To begin with, buy some line in diameters 0.10, 0.12, 014, 0.16 and 0.18mm. With these high-tech lines, such a selection will give you a spread of breaking strains, from about 2lb to about 5lb. If your fishing includes fine-line canal, river or lake work then you will need finer diameters such as 0.08mm or even 0.06mm. Margin fishing with very strong elastics demands much stronger lines; for this sort of activity, you will need line in diameters 0.20 to 0.25mm.

This will also give you some hook link line as well for tying your hooks to. It is vital to match your line and hook link to the elastic that you are using, and to match the strength of the elastic, line and hook to the size of fish that you are targeting. In your rig there has to be a weak point that will break if you get snagged or broken by a fish. That weak point must be your hook link. Never be tempted to massively uprate your line and elastic – you might just find that your pole becomes the weak point, and breaks.

Hooks

Which Hook?

There is a simple principle regarding which hook to use: match the hook to the bait (having matched the bait to the fish). A tiny bait such as a pinkie will need a tiny hook, while a grain of sweetcorn will need a much bigger one; this is logical, of course, since you are hoping to catch a much bigger fish on the grain of sweetcorn than on a tiny pinkie.

Again, you need to consider the importance of balance. The hook is balanced to the line, which in turn is balanced to the elastic. The rig will lack the power to set the hook if the hook is too big for the rest of the set-up; conversely, an ultra-fine hook will pull out or straighten when used with a powerful set-up.

For fine-line fishing for small fish, using baits such as pinkies, maggots and casters, look for fine-wire small hooks. When you step up to baits such as pellet, corn and small pellets of meat or bread for bigger fish, you will need bigger, stronger hooks. Finally, larger pieces of meat and paste need the biggest and strongest hooks of all.

The design of hooks is a compromise between hooking power and holding power. A longer shank helps a hook get a better hold. A shorter shank stays in better once you have hooked the fish. For small fish, err on the side of longer shanks, which are also easier to handle. For bigger fish, it is worth sacrificing hooking power for a good hook hold. Fine-wire hooks can act like

Selection of hooks covering stillwaters (top row), rivers (middle row), and canals (bottom row).

a cheese cutter and thicker-wire hooks therefore gain a better hook hold, but a heavier hook can hinder bait presentation. Hook choice is a varying compromise between holding power and bait presentation.

In addition, hooks that have an incurved point have the best hook hold of all, and this type of hook has become very popular in recent years for pole fishing. Although the incurved point also sacrifices hooking power, the direct connection of lifting into a fish when pole fishing overcomes this disadvantage, making this the ultimate hook type to use when fishing for carp on the pole.

Most commercial waters and many club stillwaters insist on barbless hooks, but on rivers, canals and drains you have the choice between barbless and barbed. There is a huge choice of hooks suitable for all types of fishing, which makes it difficult to know what pattern to use. The secret is to use a small selection that will cover the styles of fishing that you do. No single pattern will do it all, and sometimes you will find that a pattern is brilliant in one size yet poor in the remainder of the range. You need to experiment until you find the hooks that suit you best.

If success is eluding you, do not be too quick to blame the hook. The fault could lie elsewhere. Does your playing technique need more expertise? Is the elastic right for the line and hook? Are you allowing too much slack, or is the elastic set much too tight?

Tying Your Own Hooks

One of the many skills worth learning when you embark on the hobby of pole fishing is how to use a hook tier to tie spade-end hooks to your hook links. By doing this you can choose what hooks and what hook link to use. Take the trouble to practise, seeking help from someone who is able to show you how, and you will soon be able to tackle any situation. Tips for good hook tying include getting the tension right as you tie the hook: too much and the line will kink and curl, too little and the knot will slip. Make sure the line comes off the inside of the shank/spade. Do not forget that you can tie eyed hooks with a hook tier (not through the eye).

You will need a means of storing the tied hook lengths if you tie them at home. Try to keep the hook lengths to a standard length, say, 6 or 8in, so that changing hook links does not alter the depth setting.

Weights

You will need the usual non-toxic shot in sizes 6, 4, 1 and BB for forming a bulk on your rigs. You will also need the smaller shot in sizes 8 and 10 as

A hook tier (top) and hook wallet (above) are essential for the pole angler.

dropper shot, and, as your pole fishing becomes more sophisticated, you will see the need for more of the small sizes in the range, even going down to the tiniest size 13. Indeed, those fishing shallow waters, and especially canals, rarely use shot above a size 8, even forming bulks with these small shot.

Two other useful variations on small shot are Styl leads and a hybrid weight that is halfway between Styls and round shot, called Stotz. Styl weights give a slower fall of the bait through the water than shot for on-the-drop fishing.

Those fishing deeper water often use olivette weights. The best of these are made of dense tungsten, which is much denser than lead. The ones that thread on the line sit more centrally than those held on with silicon rubber. They are especially useful for river fishing. A selection from 0.5g to 4g or more will cover most eventualities.

Other Bits and Pieces

Pole Winders
You will need a good selection of pole winders, which should be matched to your floats. Ensure that they are wide enough and long enough to

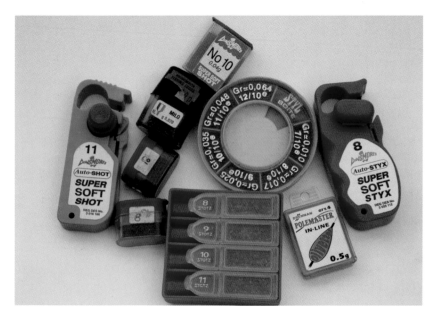

A good variety of small weights is essential to fine-tune rigs for optimum use: tiny split shot, Styl and Stotz weights are all useful. Olivettes make a neat bulk.

Shot, Styl and Stotz Weights

Shot size	Grams	Shot/Stotz Size	Grams	Styl	Grams
SSG	1.8	8	0.063	20 (for reference)	0.258
AAA	0.8	9	0.049	18 (for reference)	0.170
BB	0.4	10	0.034	16 (for reference)	0.130
1	0.24	11	0.26	14 (for reference)	0.084
4	0.17	12	0.020	12	0.064
6	0.10	13	0.012	11	0.048
				10	0.036
				9	0.025
				8	0.017
				7	0.010

Note:

1. Shot sizes of SSG down to 6 are made from non-toxic metals that are less dense than lead and actual weights are greater than those shown but the effect is the same.

2. Styl leads in original sizes 20 to 14 are illegal but floats may be marked with these weights so conversion is useful. Be aware that half Styl weights are also available, and these are even smaller than the normal sizes being 10/5 = 0.035g through to 14 = 0.004g.

accommodate the floats on the rigs preventing damage to your floats. Some winders specially fit the trays in seat boxes and some have a sliding clip to hook the loop around, removing the need for a pole winder anchor. Winder anchors are short lengths of rubber with an anchor one end and a loop the other to secure the end of the rig. Rigs are hooked on to the winder, wound around – not so tight as to cause severe kinks in the line – and then fixed to the winder by the loop. You can make your own with short lengths of old pole elastic.

Plummets

A plummet is essential for establishing the depth of the water (*see* pages 87–8), and most top pole anglers carry a selection as well as spares. Some plummets clip on the hook, others are fixed by threading the hook through a loop

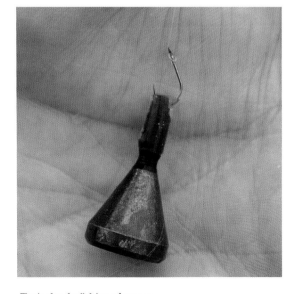

Typical pole fishing plummet.

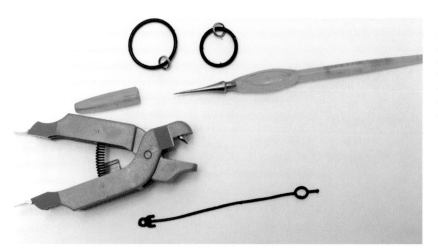

'O' rings are useful for hooking up rigs when top sets are not in use. Shot pliers help move and remove shot. The knot picker can remove tangles. Pole anchors secure rigs on winders.

A pole roller is essential for using a pole at more than 7m; for 13m or more, use two rollers, as shown here.

A pole sock is perfect for holding the end of the unshipped pole.

and then inserted into a cork on the base. A small plummet is ideal for shallow stillwater work whereas on a deeper powerful river you will need a much heavier one. There are also flat-based ones that will not sink into soft silt. The flat ones are usually fixed by inserting the hook through the loop on a short stem and then securing with a slip of silicon tubing.

Useful Tools

You never know when you will need to replace your pole elastic. It can snap at any time, including while fishing, so be sure to carry an elastic threader, spare elastic, spare Stonfo connectors and pole elastic lubricant. Disgorgers are cheap enough so it is a good idea to carry several of these in different sizes. For trimming rigs, sorting out tangles and adjusting shotting, a small pair of scissors, a Levapiombo (shot remover), a small knife, and a knot picker will prove invaluable. When storing made-up top sets with rigs attached it is useful to have a hook-up on the pole section to tether the hook. Commercially available ones are made from 'O' rings or moulded rubber, or you can make your own from a loop of old pole elastic.

Pole Rollers

A pole roller is essential for fishing at more than about 6m. As you progress to fishing a pole at

longer lengths you will find it necessary to have some means of supporting the pole as you ship it back. If you are only fishing at up to 7m, you can use your rod holdall laid sideways to support the pole, but beyond this length you definitely need a roller. There are several variations of these – some are V-shaped and others are horizontal with vertical ends. If you fish a pole at more than14m, you will need a second roller to support the pole. The V-shaped rollers come on a tripod and the flat ones on a four-legged support. Both have adjustable legs and are invaluable.

To stop the pole rolling forward into the water when you have the top sections detached there are a couple of useful gadgets that will hold the end of the pole. One is a tulip-head-shaped plastic grip, into which the pole is gently pushed, the other a device like a 5in landing net, inside which the end of the pole sits (pole sock). These are essential if you fish a water that has a high bank behind you.

Aids to Feeding

While you can feed the swim by hand when pole fishing there are several useful aids that can increase accuracy. Catapults have been around for many years, and special low-powered ones are ideal for pole fishing. The idea of attaching a small plastic cup to the end section of the pole is also well known. Originally home-made – by

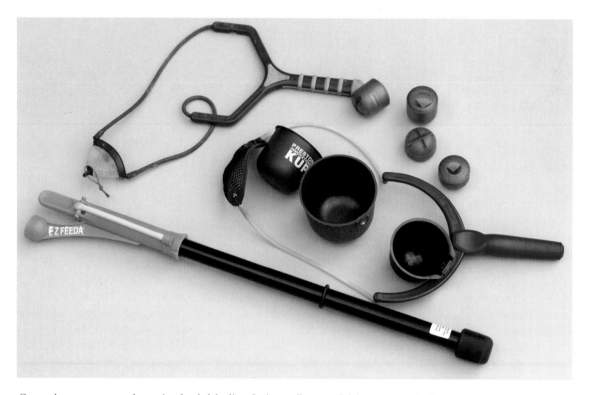

Catapults, pots, cups and a spring-loaded feeding device – all are useful for accurate feeding.

recycling items such as aerosol tops and Kinder egg containers – it is now possible to choose from a wide variety of the purpose-made ones that are available in tackle shops. Clip them on or secure them with elastic. A pole cup will give you remarkably accurate feeding and they are to be recommended.

With a larger pole pot attached to the end of a special strengthened top three set, you will be able to accurately place balls of groundbait.

Other bits and pieces related to feeding and bait include the many associated containers and gadgets (bread punches, meat punches, ground-bait bowls, bait waiters and bait boxes).

6 GETTING STARTED WITH A POLE

Pole fishing is a simple method, and that's exactly how we're going to keep it – straightforward and uncomplicated.

Let's Go Pole Fishing

Finding Somewhere to Fish

Now you are fully equipped, it is time to find somewhere to fish. Whether you go for a true 'commercial' or a club water, it is vital to select a stillwater venue that will be easy to fish for your first venture with a pole. More essentially, the water must contain plenty of small fish. They do not have to be carp; roach, rudd, perch and small bream (collectively known as 'silver fish') are all fine. If there are carp present then it is best to tackle small ones (of less than a couple of pounds). This is all about learning to walk before you try to run.

Before starting fishing ensure that you have the required day ticket or club permit and a

Check the rules regarding hooks, baits and nets before starting fishing.

This swim at Witherington Farm fishery is an ideal pitch. It is level with a platform. There are no overhanging trees or nearby power cables and the depth is a comfortable 5ft. There are plenty of fish too.

Overhead Power Cables: Look Out, Look Up!

- Never fish within 30m of any electric power lines.
- Never forget you can be electrocuted even if your rod or pole does not actually touch a power line.
- Look out for warning signs like the one opposite.
- Especially beware cables on drains and canals as the cables may be hidden in trees, or run alongside the water.

valid Environment Agency rod licence. Read the fishery rules so that you are familiar with the permitted baits and methods; be prepared to read a lengthy list of what baits and methods are banned on some fisheries!

Next, you need to find a level area of bank to put your seat on. The swim should have a depth of 5–6ft within 15ft of the bank and, most importantly, the fish should be within that range. This is where obtaining some local expert advice, perhaps from the fishery bailiff or owner, will save you a lot of time. Make it clear what you are trying to do; it is essential that the swim you are going to fish is neither too deep nor shallow, that it is free from hazards such as bushes and

The warnings are clear enough – ignore them at your peril!

weedbeds, and, vitally, that it will offer you the chance of plenty of bites from small fish. It will be better still if the bank is level, perhaps with a sturdy platform on which to set up your kit.

Your first attempts will be much easier on a dry day between April and October that is on the warm side (preferably not scorching hot), with no more than a slight breeze.

Bait

A pint of maggots is one option for this initial attempt. Again, listen to advice from those who know the water, and remember that you are trying to catch just a few fish, not the biggest or the most – that will come later! A small tin of sweetcorn or a pot of hookable (soft) pellets with a bag of feed pellets may be a better option. This is because maggots are indiscriminate as a bait and you may find that all you get are miniscule tiddlers; sweetcorn should catch better fish.

Get Comfortable

Once you have found your ideal pitch – no trees overhead, no overhead power lines within 30 yards – set your box down gently on the ground

about a foot from the front edge of the bank or platform. Make sure that the ground at the front of the bank is level so that you can, if necessary, stand on it safely. If you have legs built into or on to your box, make sure you get the top of the box level so that your feet are flat on the ground, with your thighs horizontal.

Next, set up your landing net within easy reach to your left (assuming you are right-handed). There is no need for a pole roller yet until you move on to fishing further out with a longer pole. On this first trip think about how to get organized so that everything is to hand. Once you get into this habit, pole fishing becomes a smooth and organized exercise. Ideally, everything you will need during the session – including disgorger, bait, spare hooks and shot, and any food and drink – should be reachable without your having to get off your box. Then, once you are fishing, you can remain seated rather than having to get up every time you catch a fish or need a tackle item. The fish in your swim will feed more confidently if disturbance is minimized.

As you are going to be concentrating on the tiny tip of a pole float it will help your eyes if

Once you are comfortable and organized, you can relax and get on with fishing.

you use an eyeshade or peaked baseball cap to reduce glare. Polarized sunglasses can help too.

With the landing net set up – and out of the way, so that you do not tread on it – it is time to start setting up the pole. *See* Chapter 4 for information on how to set up the pole tips with elastic; you should have a tip set up with No. 5 elastic that has a Stonfo attached, and tensioned so that the elastic goes back inside the pole when you release it after pulling it out. It should have a drop or two of lubricant at the bush. Step up to the No. 8 elastic if local advice is that you are likely to get fish over a pound on your chosen water. Set up the pole with just the top three sections. This should give you about 4m of pole; if not, add another section. Put the next two sections safely to one side where you will not tread on them or drop them in the lake.

Making a Rig

Assuming at this point that you have no ready-made pole rigs, it is time to make one on the bank. With the top rigged with a No. 5 elastic, take your spool of 0.12mm line (if using the No. 8 elastic, substitute 0.14mm line) and start by tying a small loop in the end using an overhand knot. Make the loop small, at about half an inch. Attach the loop to the Stonfo by pulling back the collar and hooking on the loop then sliding back the collar. It should now be securely attached to the Stonfo.

Run line off the spool in line with the pole until the length of line is about a foot short of the end of the pole. You should now have a length of line that is about 3.5m. Select a float taking about 0.5g and thread the end of the line through the wire eye on the side of the float, then through a couple of pieces of pole float rubber that are tight enough to prevent the float from slipping, but not too tight that you cannot alter the depth without putting undue strain on the line. Until you are more experienced, work on the basis that a float takes 0.30g for every 3ft of depth. Push the float 5ft up the line and then, after wetting the stem of the float, carefully slide on the float rubbers, with one immediately under the body of the float and the other at the extreme end of the stem. Now tie another small loop in the end of the line below the float so that the overall length of line is about 18in less than that of the pole. Again, keep the loop to half an inch.

You now need a hook link of line that is the next diameter down from your main line: if your main line is 0.12mm, use 0.10mm, if it is 0.14mm, use 0.12mm, and so on. You need to tie a suitable hook to the hook link. For maggots a barbless size 20 or 18 is about right; hookable pellets are best on a size 16 or 14, again barbless, as is sweetcorn. These hook sizes are starting points, and with more experience you can try other variations. With fishing there is no magic answer, and what works one day may fail another; you need to be prepared to experiment and understand that changing conditions and the mood of the fish themselves will dictate changes in your tactics.

The hook link needs to be about 1ft long. Many serious pole anglers use even shorter hook links, down to 6in, the idea being that no shot are placed on the actual hook link. At this stage in learning to pole fish there is no need to be so precise.

If you do not feel confident enough to be tying small spade-end hooks on the bank, you can obtain hooks that are ready-tied to nylon. The various sizes are all available in packets, tied to 0.10mm line (slightly thicker for the bigger hooks), usually a length of about 20in. Make sure the ones you buy are barbless.

Plumbing the Depth

Before shotting up the float it is a good idea to plumb the depth of the swim. This will give you a mental picture of the underwater contours of

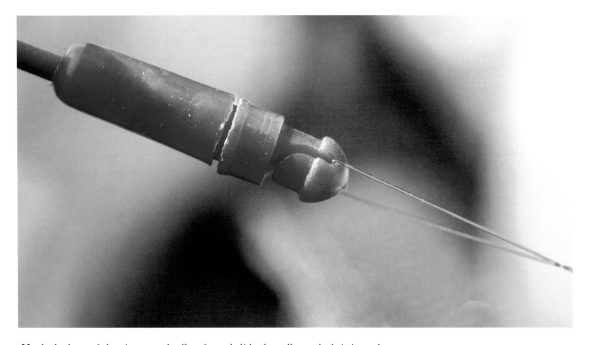

Hook the loop of the rig on to the Stonfo and slide the collar to lock it into place.

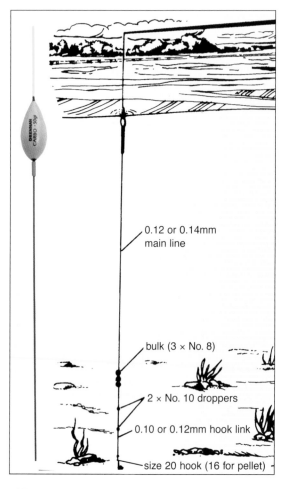

0.12 or 0.14mm
main line

bulk (3 × No. 8)

2 × No. 10 droppers

0.10 or 0.12mm hook link

size 20 hook (16 for pellet)

A basic pole fishing rig, ideal as a starting point.

the swim and prevent your getting any nasty surprises. Sometimes, after carefully shotting the float, you find that the rig is totally unsuitable for a swim because the water is actually much deeper or shallower than you expected. Attach a plummet to the hook. To plumb the depth, carefully lower the plummet into the water under the tip of the pole until you feel it hit bottom; the line should then slacken.

If at this point the float is still above the water, you have got the float set too deep; alternatively, it may disappear underwater because it is set too shallow. Estimate how much it is either above or below the water's surface and adjust the float, taking care not to damage the line (if necessary, remove the float rubbers to move the float).

Having got the exact depth directly under the pole tip try a little further out, and a little closer in. Does the depth change? Or is it fairly constant? What about to the left or right? Build a picture in your mind of whether it is level on the bottom or whether there is a slope, or a slope that levels off. If it is a slope that levels off, make a note of where this is as it will be a potential hotspot.

Provided there have been no surprises in plumbing the depth – that is to say, it is not over 10ft deep or less than 3ft – you can set the float to the exact depth. Consider moving to another swim if the depth is outside the ideal range of 5–6ft, which is easily checked now you are set up.

There are a variety of plummets available; some clip on, others are hooked on. Heavy ones are useful on rivers or where the bottom is hard gravel, and are easier to use in some respects. Light ones are less intrusive and useful in that they do not sink in silt.

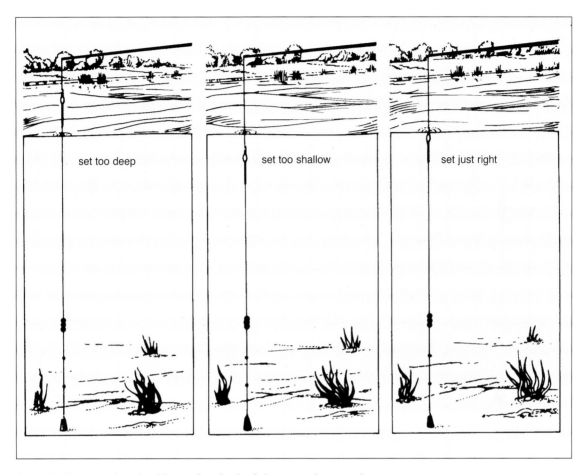

| set too deep | set too shallow | set just right |

Keep the line taut when plumbing so that the depth is measured accurately.

Apart from this mental picture of what the underwater contours of the swim are like, this plumbing exercise will also ensure that you are fishing in an effective way. If you leave it to guesswork, it is all too easy to end up fishing with 3ft of line on the bottom, wondering why the float will not settle properly, or why any bites are failing to register. There are occasions when it is useful to fish with float rigs set deeper than the swim but to catch small fish the bites will be far more frequent if the rig is set to the exact depth, or slightly less.

Shotting the Float

The next job is to shot the line so that the float rides on the surface correctly. The easiest start-ing point is a group of No. 8 shot, known as the 'bulk', that is the main shotting load plus a couple of tiny dropper shot. Place one about 8in from the hook and another one 8in above that. Then, using No. 6 shot, create a bulk about 8in above that. You will need to test the float so that, when it has settled, half an inch of bristle is showing. As you become more experienced you can fine-tune this, and in some circumstances this may be dotted (leaving barely 1mm showing) right down. You may need to add No. 8 or No. 10 shot to the bulk to get this absolutely right.

You are now ready to fish. Or are you? Looking at how you are now rigged up, you have about 6–7ft of line between the pole tip and the float. Pole fishing is generally considered

At short lengths hold the pole so that it is under your forearm.

to be all about keeping this length of line to an absolute minimum, but in this case you have two choices: keep it as it is, realizing that it is far from perfect but it does give you the versatility to fish a bit further out; or consider whether you could remove a pole section and shorten the rig at the pole end, so that there is 3ft or so less line between the tip and float, but still at least 2ft there. As the pole has been shortened this would reduce your effective fishing range and you would have to add sections. (For more on this, *see* Chapter 7.) Despite its disadvantages, you would be advised to stick to the simple rig as it is.

It is worth keeping a couple of spare sections (already joined together) handy behind you, ready to put on in case you hook a big fish. Take care to put them in a place where they will not slide into the lake and where no one can tread on them!

Regular Feeding

Bait the hook and with a gentle underhand swing drop the tackle into the water in the spot that you plumbed. It is vital to persevere with this spot. The aim is to build up a feeding hotspot in the swim, and you will not do that by casting here, there and everywhere. More importantly, you will not do it by feeding here, there and everywhere.

Assuming that you have either a pint of maggots or a kilo bag of 3mm pellets to feed, that represents at least 3,000 individual particles. In five hours' fishing you should be aiming, at least until you are really experienced, to feed at least once a minute, or 300 times in total. If you feed eight to ten maggots or pellets once a minute you will have at least fed very regularly, and probably 295 times more than the average angler. This regularity is mastered by all top match anglers, who understand how much and how often to feed through lots of practice, lots of experience and experimentation, and constantly learning from each other.

The importance of the skill of feeding cannot be overstated, and it is only through practice and experimentation that you will improve it. You do need to persevere with feeding so that the fish have time to respond; once they do, you must keep up that regularity. Keep the feed to a tightly defined area. You are fishing about 12ft from the bank, and this can be done by hand. Feed the

Keep the feed going in regularly – at short range like this it is easy to feed by hand.

Let the elastic tire the fish and when ready draw the fish over the net.

same spot every time and try to bunch the feed into an area of less than 3ft in diameter.

Action!

Getting Bites

If all goes to plan you should start to get some bites. Do not be impatient. It will take a while for your regular feeding to take effect. Position the pole tip in a way that there is not too much slack line, so that when you strike it is easy to hit the bites. Again, this will take practice. When you get on to the short-line/long-pole technique, this part will get easier even if the playing of the fish is trickier.

In striking the bites the aim is to strike hard enough to lift the float just out of the water, and no more. After a while you should start to hook fish. Having done so let the elastic do the work. You will see the elastic being pulled out of the pole. It should quickly tire the fish and, if you slowly raise the pole, allow the fish to be either swung in if the fish is small (say, under 4oz and about 7in in length), or into netting range (about 6ft from the bank and under control on

the surface). When the fish is played out, reach for the net with your left hand, at the same time keeping tension on the line (and fish) with the pole. Push the net out with the frame and mesh already sunk, taking care not to scare the fish. Keep the net still and sunk below the surface, draw the fish over it, then raise the net until the fish lies in the bottom of the mesh. Remember, always bring fish to net and not net to fish. You may find it practical to unhook the fish in the net and simply sink the net back in the water to allow it to swim away.

If your bite registration is good and your strikes timely, the fish you land should be hooked in the lip. Hold the fish gently but firmly in one hand and gently remove the hook by easing it in the opposite direction to the point of the hook. As it is barbless this should be simple. If the hook is inside the mouth of the fish and you cannot reach it, you will need to use a disgorger. The easiest type to use is the barrel type, which has a small barrel with a slot for the line. Keeping the line taut, slide the disgorger on to the line and down on to the bend of the hook. Push gently on the bend just sufficiently to dislodge the hook and remove it from

The barrel-type disgorger is ideal for the hooks that are typically used when pole fishing. These come in three sizes – use the best one for the job according to hook size.

the fish's mouth. While doing all of this, tuck the pole under your right elbow, to save putting it down.

What Have You Caught?

As you catch each fish have a look at it and see if you can identify it. Some are easy – such as tench with their olive coloration, tiny scales and little red eye, or perch with their dark bands and spiky fins. Initially you may find it harder to distinguish between roach and rudd, which have similar red fins; the roach has a down-pointing mouth and silvery sides, whereas the rudd has an upturned mouth and golden flanks. Carp come in a number of variations: fully scaled with regular scaling is a common carp; a row or two of large mirror-like scales along the back and central body (lateral line) indicates a mirror carp; those with a leather-like skin are leather carp. You may come across variations of koi carp, usually with bright or metallic coloration and often known as ghost carp.

Once you have identified your fish, gently slip it back into the water.

You will find that the different species bite differently and may be at different levels in the swim. Rudd often bite almost as soon as the bait hits the surface, carp and roach will bite at all levels, and tench, bream and crucians will be found mostly on the bottom. There are no hard and fast rules about this, and later chapters will explore how to catch fish well off the bottom. While fishing, look for tell-tale signs of fish in the swim – rises and swirls on the surface, or little patches of small bubbles coming to the surface. If you have been catching small fish for two or three hours on maggots and this happens, consider changing to a bigger hook and using sweetcorn or pellet. Start feeding some pellets or a couple of grains of corn every cast, and do not be surprised if you hook a bigger fish! Sweetcorn is weighty enough to affect the shotting of the float so you may need to remove a small shot.

Detecting Bites

Learning how to detect bites takes experience. The easiest to see and hit are the bites when the float steadily submerges. Sometimes, the float will only submerge a little more so that the bristle is still above water; you may want to see the bite develop more before striking. At other times the bristle will lift in the water; this is caused by the biting fish lifting the last shot, and is worth striking. Sometimes you will get bites before the float has settled, as if the float is undershotted. When you strike bites like this do not be surprised if you find the fish is some way off the bottom. At first, you will miss plenty of bites, perhaps not even seeing some. Check the maggot hook bait each time; if it is still untouched, it is all right to use again, but if it looks chewed you should replace it.

If you are getting bites without seeing the registration on the float check that the float is shotted down correctly, with just half an inch of the bristle showing, and try moving the last shot closer to the hook. If you are missing bites, try moving the last shot further away from the hook and ensure that you are keeping the line reasonably taut between float and pole tip.

Tangles!

All anglers, whatever their level of experience, get tangles. Welcome to the club! It is good advice to keep the rig simple to try to avoid tangles, but jerky technique, the vagaries of breezes and, especially, fish falling off the hook will all ensure that you get your fair share of the problem.

When you get a tangle, remain calm; a high proportion can be untangled quickly, provided you do not pull the knots tight, so try to loosen tangles as much as possible before methodically trying to unravel them. Sometimes you have such a 'bird's nest' that retackling is the only way to get back fishing. You will need to retrace your steps to make a new rig (see page 86). Note how many shot were required to form the bulk and droppers as this can save time. Re-plumb the depth, and if you had subsequently adjusted the depth re-make that adjustment too. Sometimes, the tangle can be unravelled but the hook length looks like a pigtail. In this case, just replace the

Jerkiness when shipping back caused this tangle, which was fortunately easily sorted.

hook length; it is vital that the hook hangs straight to achieve good bait presentation and also to assist striking.

The best way to avoid tangles is to have a smooth technique. It takes practice to eliminate all those jerks and jolts; initially, you need to take your time and fish in an unhurried, calm way. Laying the rig on the water in a line will prevent some tangles, which often occur if you dump the rig in a pile on the water. If a fish drops off (and plenty will!) it can pay to do a quick, hard cast back on the water, to straighten the rig out before it has a chance to tangle. Again, this takes practice, and it is another reason not to fish under a tree when just starting.

Experimentation

Now you know the basics of fishing with a pole, but there is plenty more to learn, and as the session progresses you may want to experiment a little. Try fishing a few inches deeper or shallower. Try moving the dropper shots up or down. After each change (and you should change only one thing at a time), try to assess the effect on the swim, and what you are catching. One thing that may happen, especially on a well-stocked commercial, is that the constant feeding of maggots (or pellets) will initially attract small roach and rudd, but, stimulated by the feeding action, other, bigger fish will turn up. In this case, consider making up a new rig with another top and stronger elastic and line.

If the session has been a success, try to have a few more sessions using similar tactics to gain confidence in the method. Do not forget the importance of balancing the tackle to the target fish, and keep the steady stream of feed going in. Each time you fish, try something a little different. If it is windy, try a float that takes more shot; if it is calm, try a lighter float. Try different swims and baits. Instead of maggots, try casters, again on a small hook.

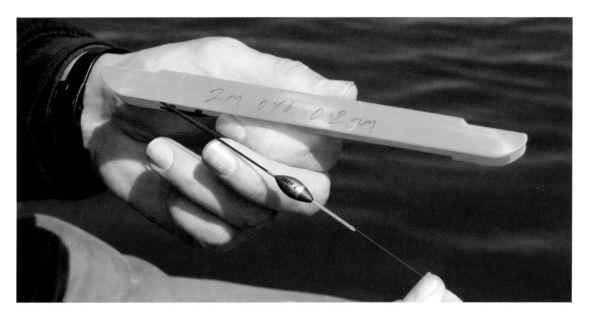

When you pack up, hook the hook on to the winder first, then wind on the rig, taking care to align the float with the deepest side of the winder. Finish by affixing the loop to the winder using either a pole anchor or the slider found on some winders.

Rigs and Winders

When you pack up for the day you can keep the rig you used on a pole winder: attach the hook to the winder then wind the rig on, taking care to align the float with the winder on the deep side, and secure the loop either with an elasticated winder anchor or with the little slider on the winder.

Label the winders so that you know what the rig is at a glance. Everyone has their own system for doing this but one tip (especially useful if you have long-line rigs for rivers) is to mark each pole section with a number using enamel paint and a fine brush, starting from the tip. Some poles are already numbered in this way. The length of the rig will then match this number. On a typical commercial fishery, you may find little variance in the length of your rigs but it will still pay at least to know how long the rigs are, and the line used. Mark the winder with details of the rig; size of float, shot load and length of rig, so that you know what it is next time.

Once you have got the hang of making up rigs at the waterside it is worth thinking about making up some at home. For top match anglers this preparation is vital, and it can save time for the casual angler. To make a suitable (and cheap) tank to test the floats, cut off the top of a 2-litre soft-drink bottle and fill it with water. This gives you a means of testing the floats, albeit with the shot right under the float. Alternatively, learn to use a Dosapiombo, which enables you try out the shot load without putting the shot on the line. Simply trap the end of the float stem in the device and add shot. It is best to fractionally undershot the rig when tank testing, and to make your final adjustments on the bank.

Once you have the shotting right, adjust the shotting and complete the rig by measuring the length of line needed for a set length of pole. If you need a rig 6ft long and the winder is 6in, then twelve winds of the winder gives the correct length; with a little homework, this method can be used for any length of rig and winder. Leave a small loop (half-inch maximum) at both ends and you can add the hook link when fishing.

7 LONG-POLE FISHING ON STILLWATERS

The Long-Pole/Short-Line Technique

Getting Started

Having started fishing the pole at its simplest, it is time to move on to the standard long-pole/short-line technique.

The secret of doing this well is to start at a modest length of pole and work up from there as you gain confidence. Taking the initial set-up of 4m of pole, and nearly as long a length of line, into long-pole/short-line fishing is simple. It will help if the swim has a flat bottom at the fishing range – if it is 5ft deep about 4m out it would be ideal if it is still the same depth at 10m out.

Assuming that the swim has a level bottom, attach the rig to the Stonfo and put the plummet on again. Take the next two joints of the pole, already joined together, and add them to the 4m of pole so that you have about 7m of pole. As before, carefully plumb the depth, this time about 7m out. To adjust the depth you will need to break the pole down again. Store the two sections of pole that you have just taken off safely behind you, where they are both in reach and unable to slide into the water.

Having done this you still have that long length of line between the pole tip and the float. Shorten this so that there is only 2ft of line between the pole tip and the float. You will see experts fishing with less than this but, until you have gained more skill in controlling the pole, it is best to try to work with the longer length. Tie another small loop in the line 2ft above the float and fix this to the Stonfo. Trim off the spare line. Your rig is now only 7–8ft long. That means that when breaking down the pole you need to take another joint off, so that you are taking off three joints. The hook should come to hand when you swing it in.

When putting the pole together only do it tightly enough to hold it securely. If you over-tighten it, you could find it hard to take apart. And make sure you align the joints carefully, otherwise you may strain and crack them. Keep the

When fishing further out you will need to break down the pole at 3m; note the use of a joint aligner on the male section of pole.

Adjust the length of line above the float when fishing, according to conditions. Make the rigs up on the long side, then, once you have plumbed up cut the length of line above the float to suit. Around 2ft is suitable when you start pole fishing. In windy conditions a longer length is more manageable.

joints clean at all times, as dirt and grit stuck to them will make them wear rapidly. Remember that you are going to be putting together and taking apart the pole very frequently, so it is vital to take care when doing so.

When shipping the rig to the swim, practise being smooth, and learn to do this without drag-

ging the bait in the water. In shipping out the rig some baits lend themselves to being trailed in the water. Maggots, casters and sweetcorn can be shipped out this way but delicate pastes, bread punch or soft hookable pellets are likely to fall off and will need greater care. Smoothness is a vital skill in pole fishing, and will help avoid tangles.

Remember to follow a steady feeding pattern, feeding once a minute with a few maggots or pellets. You will notice that you are now in much closer contact with your float. This gives you two big advantages and one drawback. First, you can strike more directly with much less line between pole and float; and second, you can control the float better. This is apparent if there is any breeze blowing. By holding the pole still, you will be holding the float against the slight surface drift, or undertow, which is where the water is moving in the opposite direction to the wind. This improves bait presentation as the feed bait is also still on the lake bed.

The disadvantage is that any unwanted pole movements, such as when you feed the swim while holding the pole, are magnified. If you are not careful, the float may be jerked out of place. This means that you need to practise holding the pole still while feeding, and when waiting for bites.

Landing Fish by Breaking Down the Pole
The big difference to the first session is that, in order to bring the fish within range of the landing net, you are going to have to break the pole down. How much you break the pole down depends on the size of the fish. When a small fish is played out the elastic will have nearly all retracted back inside the pole, so breaking down the pole at the same point as for re-baiting will bring the fish into net range.

With a bigger fish, say, 2 or 3lb or more, there may be several feet of elastic still protruding from the end of the pole, and you will need to determine where to break the pole down to get the fish within netting range. There is no hard and fast rule; it comes from experience in understanding the stretch in the elastic you are using and its effect on the fight of the fish. In this session, you have been adding/removing three joints to fish and re-bait. When landing fish you might find that for small fish you need to remove all three joints, while for bigger fish you need to remove only two joints. If the elastic is a little on the soft side for the fish you are catching you might find that you need to remove

just one joint, or, indeed, none of the joints. In this case consider taking the rig off and putting a different pole top set on with stronger elastic (the next size up that you have).

Playing Fish
You can use the longer pole to your advantage when playing fish, since it gives you more leverage to guide the fish away from the feeding area and snags. Furthermore, you can add joints when playing a fish. With the short pole to hand method you have little choice but to lift the pole high. When playing the fish with a longer pole you should keep the pole low, and with a shorter line to the float it is much easier to do this, until it is time to net the fish. This makes a huge difference to how hard fish pull back, especially carp. It is vital that the elastic tires the fish, and you need to keep some pressure on it to do this. But sometimes when you hook bigger fish you will find that it is vital to add joints quickly and smoothly, to allow the fish to run.

When adding joints to the pole with a fish pulling hard on the other end, take care to align the joints. It is possible to split a joint if it is only partly home and the fish suddenly pulls the pole round. Practice is vital – the more fish you play and land, the more confident and competent you should become.

Avoid Losing Fish
In your early pole-fishing days you may find yourself losing a high proportion of the fish you hook. There are several possible reasons.

Elastic Set Too Tight or Too Heavy in Use
When you pull the elastic out of the pole it should retract slowly rather than being under massive tension when you pull on it. Try slackening it off by a turn on the bung.

The idea of elastic is that it should act as a shock absorber that quickly plays the fish, but it is tempting to substantially increase the size of elastic in the belief that you will land fish more quickly. Taken to extremes, this may result in insufficient stretch for the hook to retain its hold, or in the line breaking. Expect the elastic to be

Let the pole elastic do the hard work of tiring the fish.

working when playing fish. It should be neither continually at full stretch nor barely emerging from the pole.

Hook too Small/Wrong Hook Pattern/Mismatched Hook

The hook-hold is your link with the hooked fish. Sometimes the hook does not match the bait, or the hook is too fine in the wire, causing the hook to spring out of the mouth of the fish. A bigger/stronger hook may do the trick. You may also consider using a different pattern.

Not Striking Hard Enough/Striking Too Hard

Striking when pole fishing is different from striking when fishing with a rod – as the length of the pole increases, so too does the effective striking length. This means that at longer lengths

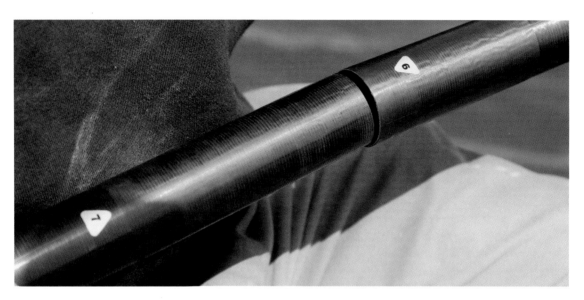

Take care to align joints exactly to prevent damage to them.

Keep the pole low when playing carp.

Dangling Elastic

If you get dangling elastic, where the Stonfo fails to retract properly or can be felt sticking as it is pulled out, try the following:

- Remove the elastic from the pole top.
- Ensure it is completely clean.
- Pre-stretch it to its maximum.
- Carefully work an elastic lubricant such as Slippery Eel or Slip into the entire length of elastic.
- Allow the inside of the pole top set to dry completely in a warm place such as an airing cupboard. Carefully pull a tiny piece of tissue paper through the pole top with strong fishing line or use a pole top cleaning kit to clean inside the pole top.
- Re-fit the elastic, lubricating the bush and tensioning the elastic slightly more than previously.
- Try to prevent water getting inside the pole top while fishing.

---

little movement is needed by the angler to set the hook – a gentle controlled lift of just 6in is ideal. Getting it right takes practice.

Poor Playing Technique
When playing a fish it is vital to keep some tension in the elastic, especially when breaking down the pole. Avoid dipping the end of the top sections as you do so, giving slack line. As you will often be using a barbless hook this is doubly vital. Again, practice and experience are key.

Feeding Options

As you go on to longer lengths of pole, feeding by hand becomes less viable, and accuracy suffers. Both catapults and pole pots have their place, and you are advised to take advantage of both.

Catapults
The small bait catapult is the easiest option for feeding. Special catapults for pole fishing have lighter elastic than those for river fishing, and

these are ideal for accurate fishing up to about 15m. The idea when pole fishing is to keep the feeding to a tight patch.

When using a catapult while holding a pole, trap the pole under your forearm against your leg, to free up both your hands. Keep your feed bait close to your left hand so that you can load the catapult single-handed and remain in control of the pole at all times. Practice will make perfect.

The advantage of using a catapult is that you do not need to ship the pole back to refill the pole pot, making it ideal for when you need very regular feeding. The disadvantage is that it may not be as accurate.

Pole Pots
For the novice, a modest pot that is large enough to take a small handful of pellets or maggots should suffice. You will need to be smooth in shipping out or you will spill the contents. It helps to only part-fill the pot, at least until you are practised in this.

The advantage of the pole pot is the unbeatable accuracy it offers. If you want to feed small quantities of bait there are also 'sprinkle pots', which let you shake out a few small pellets when required. Use the pot every time you ship out, and maintain the regular feeding.

Varying the Presentation

On the Drop
There is more to pole fishing than simply always doing it the same way, hard on the bottom. Your basic rig had a small bulk plus two droppers. If your feeding was constant, you may have noticed that some of the bites were coming before the float had settled properly, in other words, 'on the drop'. Sometimes the fish are so keen that you start to get swirls as the fish take the pellets or maggots just under the surface. What would happen if you were to try a slightly different rig? Store the rig you have been using on a pole winder and make up a new rig, this time with a smaller float, taking the equivalent of a No. 8 shot for each foot of depth. The ideal float for

Learn to use a catapult when holding the long pole. It takes practice and the right sort of catapult. This type of catapult can be loaded with your free hand while holding the pole with the other. (Photo: Stu Dexter)

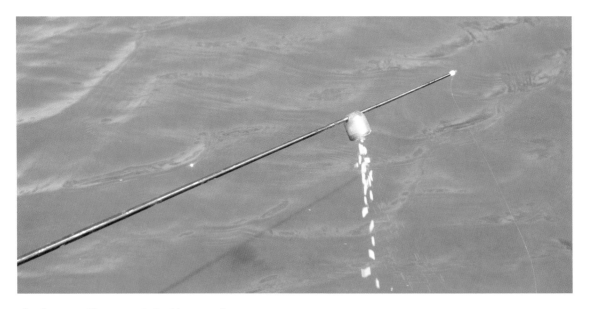

A pole pot enables you to feed with tremendous accuracy.

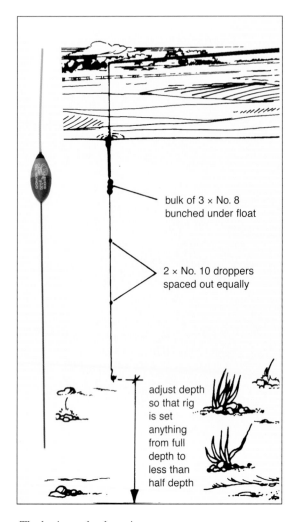

bulk of 3 × No. 8
bunched under float

2 × No. 10 droppers
spaced out equally

adjust depth
so that rig
is set
anything
from full
depth to
less than
half depth

The basic on-the-drop rig.

this has a slim body. It will be much easier to fish with this light rig if there is hardly any wind.

This time, when shotting up it is important to spread the shot down the line. Put one No. 8 right under the float, then the next No. 8 a foot below that, and the next one another foot below that, and the next one another foot below. Assuming you have a swim 5ft deep, this leaves 2ft of line below the last shot. Put a No. 10 shot a foot from the hook. Check the float/shotting. To trim the float so that just a little of the float tip is showing should only take another No. 10 or two, and these should be put underneath the

float. You now have a rig that, when laid on the water in a line, will give you a slow sinking bait.

Keep up the steady feeding, start fishing with the new rig and watch the float like a hawk when it is settling. It may bob, lift or slide away. You may find your catch rate improving. You are now fishing a variation of your original rig – you are still fishing the full depth of the swim but with the bonus of trying to catch some of the fish that are intercepting your loose feed as it drops through the water. This method of presentation is in itself useful, and now you have two basic methods of float fishing.

This shotting pattern is just a starting point. It is easy to see that by moving shot on the line, and varying the size of the shot, you can change the rate at which the bait falls through the water. Using a float that takes a smaller shot load and using No. 10s instead of No. 8s will give a slower rate of fall. Moving more shot under the float will also do this, although if you fish a float (attached top and bottom) with too much shot under the float it can be prone to tangling (not that this should stop you trying the method). In this instance it may be better to change to a smaller float. To slow the rate of fall yet further, consider using Styl leads or Stotz.

When fishing this style you will notice that when striking the bites you make contact with the fish in mid-water. In other words, the fish are feeding well off the bottom and this is a good time for further experimentation.

Fishing Up in the Water
Start by shallowing up by 2ft. Move the extra shot up under the float. Provided you can maintain the constant steady feeding, you should still be catching fish. Try changing to a smaller float with smaller shot only, say, No. 10s or less. From here on, it is down to you to experiment. There are all sorts of rigs that can work, and you can catch carp, rudd, roach, and even bream by fishing just under the surface. Experiment with feeding, depth, hooks and shotting. Remember that when you are catching like this you will need to vary your tactics as the session progresses and the fish vary the ways in which they feed.

Set depth of rig to less than half depth. Experiment to find best depth

3 × No. 10 spread out

3 × No. 10 bulked together

Two simple rigs for fishing up in the water.

Watch out for the swim getting so worked up that you start to get lots of fast bites that are difficult to hit; you may start to foul-hook fish too. If this happens, you need to calm the swim down a little. Try feeding more heavily but slightly less regularly. Try feeding in a less tight pattern, spreading the feed around. Try fishing on the edge of the feed area. Whatever happens, experiment with some different tactics – a swim full of boiling activity and fast unhittable bites can be very frustrating!

Once again it may be necessary to shorten the line between float and pole tip. You could end up with a total rig length of less than 4ft. Although the very short line improves your striking into the fish there is a danger that, with the fish right under the pole tip, it will scare them. To get around this, consider lengthening the rig so that there is more line (as much as 5ft) above the float. To do this you will need to make a new rig. Fish it so that the rig is well away from the pole tip. Accept that what you have lost in control and direct contact with the rig should be

compensated for with bigger catches from much less wary fish.

Both of the options will work on their day – you just need to experiment to see which is best.

In match conditions it may be necessary to fish at full length – 14m or more – to get away from competing anglers with this deadly summer method. Some top anglers 'tap' the surface of the water to fool the carp into thinking there is free bait going in, although the only bait is the hook bait. This method is barred at some venues.

Laying On

Fishing with the bait hard on the bottom is an effective method for bigger fish. Big roach, especially, need time to look at your bait, and fishing caster on the bottom can be a good way to catch them. However, it is more likely that you will be targeting carp with this method. This laying-on style is useful if you have an island swim in reach of your pole. Carp like to keep tight to features such as these, and this is where dibber floats are useful. It may be shallow in the shadow of the reeds on an island but the ability to fish with little fuss and great accuracy can pay off. *See* Chapter 8 for more details on methods for this.

Placing the Rig

As with any other form of float fishing, the way you place your rig in the water affects the way the rig will fish. There are several options. For on-the-drop fishing, the usual way is to lay the rig on the water in a straight line to the side. For fishing on the bottom, a controlled lowering of the rig is favoured by many top anglers. This stops the bait floating back upwards as the rig sinks, causing tangles.

Tactical Considerations

Drift and Undertow

Although it is recommended that you learn to pole fish in calm conditions, the British weather means that you will often be contending with wind and its effects on the water. The long-pole angler needs to be aware of two of these effects:

1. First, the pole will be more difficult to handle, especially in gusty conditions. In strong winds you may be unable to use the pole at all, either because you will not be able to hold it still enough to control the float, or because there will be a danger of breaking the pole.
2. The water itself will be affected, usually by surface drift. Although there may be a drift on the surface, the water underneath may not be moving in the same way. If you let your float drift, your hook bait will drag through the swim, behaving differently from your loose feed and making the fish suspicious of your hook bait.

All that water moving in one direction has to go somewhere, and if the wind blows long enough you may find that the surface water turns over when it reaches the bank, and the deeper water moves in the opposite direction to the wind. This gives three potential outcomes: surface drift in the direction of the wind; undertow against the wind; and surface drift with the wind with an opposing undertow. It is certainly complex. Whichever one it is – and it can change by the minute in strength, direction and combination – you are going to have to keep track so that you can present your bait well and take into consideration where your bait is ending up.

Provided the wind is not too strong, you should be able to hold the float steady. Drift and undertow have another effect when fishing a bait on the bottom. They will be trying to pull the line and sink the float, and you will need a float with a thicker tip to counteract this.

The wind can also catch the line. One way of trying to stop it from pulling on the float is to have a shot on the line above the float. Exactly how big a shot and where to place it is up to you, but do not be afraid to have a shot of as large a size as AAA – it will not affect the shotting of the float provided it is at least a foot from the float. That means you need at least 2ft of line above the float.

An alternative method of shotting above the float is to have a single No. 10 shot on the line. This can be moved much closer to the float to steady the line. This will affect the float but can be used to your advantage. To do this the float is shotted in a way so that when the extra shot is in effect (near the float), the float is nearly dotted. The shot can then be moved during the session to alter the trim of the float – the amount of tip showing – according to the prevailing conditions. This is ideal on blustery days when the wind strength is frequently changing, and the lake's surface is varying from calm to ruffled to rippled.

Feeding

Generally, a frequent, regular but sparse feeding of the swim is recommended. There is nothing wrong with this but when a shoal of ravenous fish is in the swim it may not be the best option. You may get short spells of catching fish that then stop for a while, and then another brief catching spell. This means that the fish are coming in for a few minutes, eating all the bait – signified by the active patches of bubbles – and then clearing

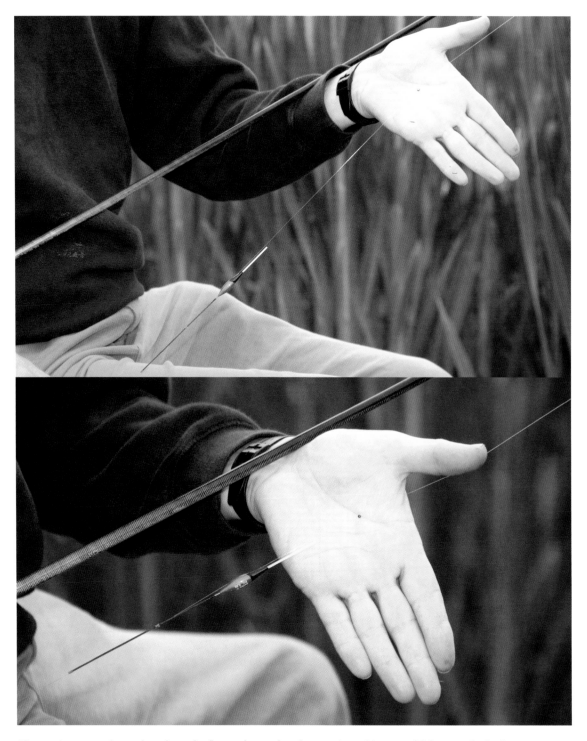

Two variants on using a shot above the float: a larger shot that can be as big as an SSG to steady the line, or a tiny No. 10 much closer to the float.

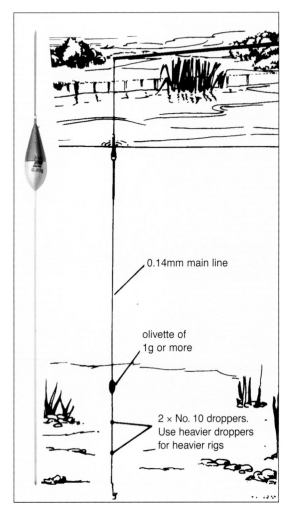

0.14mm main line

olivette of
1g or more

2 × No. 10 droppers.
Use heavier droppers
for heavier rigs

*For deep water a simple bulk down rig is a good
starting point.*

swim can change from the fish feeding tentatively to the fish feeding with a frenzy.

Deep-Water Considerations
While most purpose-built commercial fisheries are shallow, there are some waters that are much deeper. In shallow water a float that takes just a few dust shot is fine but, as the depth increases, so does the need for more weight. If only it were as simple as doubling the shot load each time you double the depth – but it is not. At modest depths this will work but as you start to get depths in excess of 8ft it is time to use tungsten olivettes and to consider substantial weight load increases. Do not be afraid to use floats that take up to 3g, as you will need to get your bait down fast. A guide to weight loads might be 1g for 8ft, then adding 0.5g for each 2ft increase in depth. You may need bigger dropper shots – try No. 8 and No. 6 shots – to register the bites more positively.

Using this type of technique in deep water, you are more likely to be fishing for bream, and the steadier presentation afforded by the heavier rig will help catch these.

Groundbaiting in Stillwaters
Traditional summer bream fishing involved lots of groundbait, usually plain breadcrumb. That method is less popular now, but there are times when groundbaiting is useful on stillwaters, and not just for bream. Carp sometimes respond well to groundbait, as do tench, and, surprisingly, roach.

Modern groundbaits are far more complex than simple breadcrumb, with additives to change their activity and attractiveness. It is usual for groundbait with a high feed content to be used in summer, a lower feed content to be used in spring and autumn, and the lowest feed content of all in winter. A summer groundbait has particles of ground bread, maize, hemp and fish meal, to name but a few of the possible ingredients, and is usually light in colour. By contrast, a winter groundbait is a carrier for a modest amount of feed such as pinkies, jokers or casters, and will be dark in colour, and possibly bulked out with leam.

off for a while. The problem is that there is only enough feed to keep them in the swim for short periods, and this is a sure sign that you need to feed more heavily. Instead of just a dozen or so pellets, try stepping up the feeding to a handful every five minutes. Gauging how much more is the tricky part, and is a case of varying the amounts and frequency of feeding according to what develops.

It is said that while the commonest feeding error is underfeeding, the second commonest is overfeeding. If you get it right, though, your

Whether you choose to use groundbait is the key question. Groundbait can be like dynamite: if you get it right, you can unlock the secrets of your swim; if you get it wrong, you can destroy it. At times, it is a case of trying it and seeing what happens. If the fish respond well, keep catching them until the bites start to dry up, and then risk introducing some more.

There are two main ways to introduce groundbait to the swim when pole fishing: throw it in using the end of the pole as a marker, or use a pole cup. Opinions are split on the best option. Those concerned about scaring the fish feel that deep water masks the splash that scares them, while in shallow water using a pot is more discreet. Others argue that fish are attracted to the splash, responding to it like a dinner gong. With some species it appears to matter little but bream in shallow water can be scared out of the swim, especially if they have yet to settle properly; in this case, it is best to err on the side of caution. Perhaps the best advice is to ball it in to attract fish to an empty swim, and cup it in when the fish are already present.

Going Longer

Once you are comfortable fishing at 7m, having got used to shipping and unshipping the pole, it is time for the next step. How long you go is your choice but you could try at least 9m, and perhaps even 11m. There is not a great deal of difference in fishing the greater length compared to 7m, except that it is too far to feed by hand, and you will need to use a catapult or pole pot. Use a pole roller rather than just resting the spare sections on your rod holdall. With a greater length of pole sticking out behind you, you need to ensure that it does not obstruct the path around the lake or get trodden on, and that it cannot roll forwards into the lake.

The most significant change, when using a longer pole, is in the way you hold it. (*See* photographs on pages 110–11.) With 7m it is easy to manage but at 11m your method needs greater consideration. Assuming you are right-handed,

the initial change is that you can rest the pole on your right thigh with your right forearm along the pole. As you increase the pole length, more support is needed. To do this, turn slightly to the right, rest the pole across both thighs and use your left hand, palm uppermost, to support the pole beyond your left knee. This method will work for up to about 14m. To do it well takes practice, favourable conditions, and, most importantly, a good sitting position, with your thighs level, your feet supported and your back straight.

With pole lengths of beyond 14m it is a question of your physical strength and technique if you want to hold the pole unaided for any length of time. If you find using the longer lengths tiring, you will need to practise at shorter lengths to build your strength and technique; observing the technique of other anglers can also help. Fortunately, however, there is another answer – fit a support known as spray or bump bars to the front legs of the foot plate on your box. This will give you the additional support that you require. Much longer lengths of pole require the use of a second pole roller; make sure you get the alignment of the two pole rollers correct to avoid stressing your pole. With much more pole to handle, the bouncing around of the end of the pole can easily lead to tangles.

Awkward Banks

A further consideration when breaking down the pole at longer lengths is whether there are obstructions behind you. The most common one is where you fish from a ledge or platform at the base of a high bank. Shipping the pole straight back is not an option. If the bank is not too high it may be possible to lift the pole over it and ship back although even this may be awkward, and will force you to keep the tip of the pole low to the water. It will be vital to keep some tension in the elastic, which is not always easy with small fish; there is a danger that the line will go slack and the fish will be allowed to escape. Try using lighter elastic than usual in these circumstances.

For pole lengths up to around 8m you can hold the pole with one hand, resting the pole along the underside of your arm and on your thigh.

At lengths longer than 8m, use both hands to steady the pole.

Sitting in a more sideways position brings both legs into play to give greater support. Ensure the height of your box is exactly right for this.

Using a spray bay and both hands in this position is another alternative when using a long pole.

When the bank behind you is angled steeply, a pole sock is vital to stop the unshipped joints sliding forward into the water.

The alternative is to break the pole down more than once; in extreme instances, this could involve removing a joint at a time, in a slow and laborious process. If the bank behind you is steep or high, you may have little choice but to do this.

In both instances the unshipped joints are likely to be steeply angled towards the water so take care to ensure that the front end is held securely with a tulip device or pole sock, even more so if unshipping more than once.

8 ADVANCED LONG-POLE FISHING ON STILLWATERS

Carp in Summer

Feeding Habits

Carp are at their most active during the warmest months of the year. From May through to October carp feed well, and consequently are the main target fish during these months on many stillwaters, especially well-stocked commercial fisheries. On that basis it ought to be easy to catch them yet it often seems more difficult than you would think.

There are two occasions when carp can prove difficult to catch in summer: first, when they are more interested in spawning than in feeding (although once they have finished spawning they are ravenous); and second, during very hot weather, when they may be easily visible but content to cruise around on the top, seemingly uninterested in feeding. This gives a clue to the ideal summer feeding temperature for carp, which is in the range of 60 to 70 degrees Fahrenheit (15 to 21 degrees Celsius). When temperatures climb above this, their willingness to feed tails off rapidly. They are much more willing to feed if conditions change to cooler weather or during the cooler times of the day,

Summer pole fishing on commercial fisheries: catching hard-fighting carp to double figures.

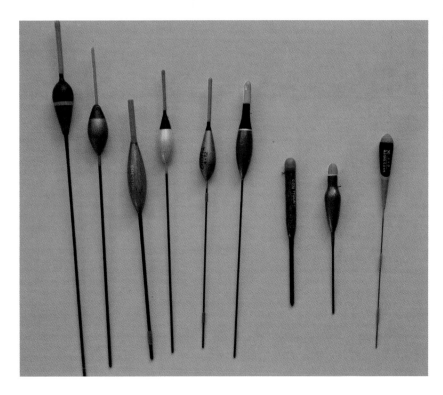

Tiny floats ideal for up-in-the-water carp and roach fishing: the thick-tipped ones are perfect for using pellets, punched meat or corn; the thin-tipped ones are best for roach, using casters.

such as early morning or late evening, or if a breeze springs up.

Another characteristic of carp is that they learn quickly, so methods and baits need to change constantly. Successful pole fishing for carp means taking a selection of bait, experimenting with rigs, and thinking hard about the way you feed them. Highly active carp will eventually find your bait in summer no matter what you do, but getting a shoal of carp to feed ravenously and lose their natural caution takes skill and patience.

In summer a shoal of good-sized feeding carp need an area to feed in that is bigger than a dinner plate. The danger when feeding a swim with a pole cup or pot is that it is easy to dump a great pile of bait into a very small area just a few inches across. The shoal of carp then tries to get to the same small pile of bait, and the pole angler has lots of carp brushing the line, causing false bites, and starts to strike at them. The result is foul-hooked fish, which is the last thing you want.

Methods for Summer Carp

Resistance to Floats

One of the great advantages of using a pole is that you can use floats that take very little weight. Experience has shown that using as light a float as possible, taking into account its visibility and ability to support the bait, gives a virtually resistance-free rig. Bites are confident sailaways rather than quick unhittable bobs. This approach can be refined, and the use of miniscule floats combined with well-thought-out feeding is a devastating method. Remember, though, that you must avoid striking those line bites that show as little knocks on the float.

The Right Gear

Active carp are fighting carp, so your gear must be balanced to the size of fish that you expect to catch. For carp to around 3lb, lines of 0.12mm and 0.14mm with size 10 elastic are fine. This gear will cope with shoal bream and tench as well. For carp running up to around 5 or 6lb, it

With practice it is possible to keep feeding the swim while a carp is being played.

is advisable to step up the gear slightly, to 0.16mm and 0.18mm lines with size 12 or 14 elastic. For carp to around 8–10lb, step up further, to 0.20mm to 0.25mm lines and size 16 or 18 elastic. Beyond that you are looking at either strong carp or margin poles with the heaviest elastic of 18, 20 or higher, and lines of 0.25mm upwards. Remember that the heaviest elastic can exert a very strong pull indeed, and when it comes to the crunch something has to give. That something must be the hook-hold or the hook itself and not the pole.

With these strong lines you will need to match the hooks – strong hooks in sizes 16 to 12 are the correct choice.

Playing the Fish
There is a great deal of skill in playing carp effectively on the pole, and there are several points worth reiterating:

- Balanced tackle is a must – pole, elastic, main line, hook length and hook – all matched, with the hook length always the weakest link.
- Keep the pole tip low until the carp is close in, then lift the pole to bring it smoothly to the surface to net it. If the carp belts off, settle it down again with gentle treatment before attempting to bring it in again. Frantic attempts to bully the fish into the net are bad for the fish, your temper and your tackle.
- Practice makes perfect, so if you made a kibosh of landing a carp, pause to think about how you could do it better next time. Quietly watch other experienced anglers, or a DVD or video to see how it is done.
- Very experienced anglers are able to continue feeding their swims at the same time as playing carp. This takes skill and practice, and is only viable if you are already feeding the swim regularly with a catapult. This means

that the rhythm of feeding remains unbroken during the times when a scrapping carp keeps you otherwise occupied.

- Sometimes, foul-hooked fish are unavoidable. Prevent potential tangles by keeping the pole low, tip in the water if possible, as you will lose most fish hooked this way. When the rig does catapult back it will be underwater, where it will not tangle.

Finding the Swims

There are at least four areas of your summer swim that could potentially produce carp:

1. The margins to either side of your peg.
2. The area 6–7m out, which is the point at which, on many commercial fisheries, the bottom levels out.

3. In open water at full pole length; this is a potential up-in-the-water swim, although there may be carp feeding on the bottom too; and
4. Depending on the layout of the lake, you may have a far bank margin swim, especially on a canal-type lake or one with islands within reach of your pole.

Resting Swims

Identifying more than one area to feed improves your chances no end. If you can get the rigs right for each spot – and that can mean having several top sets rigged up, plus a margin pole – the method of feeding several spots simultaneously means that you can alternate between them. This gives the fish a chance to settle and feed undisturbed. Then, when you do finally try a margin swim (or swims, as you could have

A swim with at least three potential areas to fish: the far bank against the island at 13m (A); mid-swim at 7m (B); and the margin to either side (C).

more than one), a big fish can be waiting for you, already feeding confidently.

A typical approach might be to fish three areas in rotation, saving the margin areas for much later in the session. Keep your eye on the baited areas for patches of bubbles, swirls or discoloration.

A feeding pattern that is so complex should not be attempted until you have at least some experience; it may pay to build up from feeding a single area to two areas, then three and, finally, four or more. Some very skilful anglers are masters of this approach, being able to switch swims at exactly the right time and rarely killing an area completely.

Alternative Baits and Approaches

One of the challenges of summer pole fishing for carp is that lots of small fish are likely to be active too. This means your soft hooker pellets can get ripped to shreds before the carp even see them. Get the carp competing strongly enough, though, and only the bravest of small rudd and roach will venture near. Until then you need a way to beat the tiddlers and this is where hard pellets are useful. You will need to attach them with a bait band, or superglue them to a piece of elastic band. This gives you a bait that the small fish will knock about as it sinks but there will be a bait left for the carp to take when it reaches the bottom.

The use of chopped luncheon meat is another devastating method, and a good alternative when the carp are wise to pellets. A more traditional approach is the use of chopped worm and caster. The juices released by the chopping are an added attraction that triggers the carp into feeding.

Margin Pole Fishing

The biggest and craftiest carp can often be found in the margins of commercial fisheries and similar lakes. They learn that, when anglers pack up in the evening, they often empty their remaining bait in the water close in, and it can be worth trying for these big fish later on, when other anglers are leaving. Use a purpose-designed margin pole, with strong elastic, line and hook, and the soft-

paste approach, which combines a big bait with matching big strong hook. A tough, long-bristled float is ideal, and you will know when the bait has gone as the float will pop up, the paste being heavy and having the effect of a shot. The size of the bait ensures that, although the little fish can peck at it, they cannot get it into their mouths. As with sweetcorn, paste is best fished dead-depth, so careful plumbing is required.

Feed the swim during the late afternoon, with big pellets such as 6 or 8mm, but leave it completely alone until later in the day. The carp get conditioned to this late feeding period and can sense that anglers are leaving the water. This is the best chance of catching the biggest carp in the lake; these are the fish that have cunningly kept well away all day. With strong tackle it is vital to use it to its best advantage when you hook a big one. You are likely to be fishing alongside reeds so you need to get the fish away from them quickly. It is often a case of swivelling around on your seat as you strike, to throw the fish off balance. You also need to be prepared for a situation in which the hooked carp belts off into open water. Certainly, it is not worth risking an expensive match pole in this hook-and-hold type of fishing.

Floating Pole for Carp

Two members of the famous Barnsley Blacks team invented the method of floating a long length of pole on the water – using extension joints, you can extend the pole to as much as 20m – using a foot of line without a float or shot, just a hook and bait. It is simplicity itself and works on a bolt-rigging principle. Using a catapult, a steady stream of bait is fired at the end of the pole; the fish, having to compete for food, rise in the water and go into a feeding frenzy. The pole signals that a fish has taken the bait by swinging left or right, with the elastic rapidly exiting the pole.

This controversial method is certainly effective but many fisheries ban it, so check first before using it.

As the pole is floating on the water it is vital to prevent water getting inside it as much as

This margin swim, just 15in deep, was fed for an hour before being tried out. Two fish of 9 and 10lb were caught quickly on sweetcorn. The carp fed eagerly, discolouring the water.

possible. Use a Stonfo that fits tight to the pole tip, an elastic base plug, which does not allow water past it into the main body of the pole, and nose cones in the lower sections for the same reason. As the pole is lying flat on the water it is best to hold the butt end as low as possible; one way is to hold it between your feet. Fish it at long lengths – 14m plus – with strong elastic.

When you get a bite, ship th e pole back along the surface of the water; do not try to lift the pole until you reach the breaking joint, otherwise you will smash it. From this point, play the fish to the net in the normal way. When shipping out with the bait dragging in the water, ensure that it is firmly attached. Baits such as sweetcorn and banded pellet are ideal.

Carp in Winter

Temperatures and Feeding

You can still catch carp in the winter, especially from heavily stocked waters, but you do need to take into account the prevailing conditions. Mild is good. That means air temperatures over 50 degrees Fahrenheit (10 degrees Celsius) in the day, and not too cold at night. A single moderate frost might not make that much difference but bitterly cold winds, daytime temperatures of just two or three degrees or less, and a succession of very hard frosts will lower the water temperature enough to make the carp sluggish at best, and practically comatose at worst.

Fish are such unpredictable creatures that there is always a chance of a red-letter day in the most surprising of conditions. The many and varied triggers that set fish off feeding are far from fully understood. There are many instances of carp feeding with abandon on semi-iced-up waters, or, conversely, refusing to feed when conditions seem ideal. By and large, however, sustained warm weather in winter, especially with mild winds, will give you a good chance of finding feeding carp.

In lower temperatures (below 45 degrees Fahrenheit, or 8 degrees Celsius) the carp may shoal tightly and stay put. The areas in which they shoal may be deeper, or they may stick in and around snaggy areas such as reed beds.

There does seem to be some critical temperature point at which the sort of bait the fish are willing to take changes. This is around 50 degrees

One way of fishing to an island is to use a floating pole, with the pole trapped between your feet.

Provided the weather is not too severe, there is a chance the carp will feed – Graham making the most of a sunny day in January.

Fahrenheit (10 degrees Celsius). Above this temperature, many types of bait will work. Below it, only baits such as maggot, caster and bloodworm are likely to tempt them, although sweetcorn can be surprisingly effective. Try stimulating the carp into feeding by introducing finely chopped sweetcorn, worm or casters. That way there is enough scent in the water to trigger a response without overfeeding the carp. Oil-based pellets become less effective in cold water, while sweet flavours such as Scopex are more effective. Try adding a couple of drops to your maggots.

This slowdown in tmetabolism means that feeding the swim must be reduced, and many winter anglers scale down their rigs to use No. 8 elastic set soft with lines of 0.10 and 0.12. Smaller hooks are necessary when using maggots, and floats should be dotted right down to increase sensitivity, for bites can be miniscule at times.

With the gentlest of lifts to set the hook it is possible to con the carp into the net before they wake up properly and realize they are hooked.

The Hook-in-the-Loop Method

The increasingly popular F1s (crucian carp crossed with carp hybrids) are reliable feeders in winter. The tricky part about catching them is in detecting the bites. In mild conditions they will feed well, and take small hookable pellets (4mm) but, even with a fine-bristled pole float, bites are tiny. Thinking angler Giles Cochrane devised an unusual method to fool them into biting more boldly. A light pole float is shotted with a bulk of No. 8s about 18in to 2ft from the hook. The hook link of 12in of 0.12mm line is tied by using a free sliding eyed hook of size 18 to 14 (according to the size of pellet) in a loop that is 2in long. The loop is tied using an overhand knot so that the hook is sliding free on the loop. The rig is completed by having two No. 8 shot as droppers bunched at the top of the loop. The rig should be fished at dead-depth with only the tip of the bristle showing. You will need to experiment – sometimes a smaller loop of 1in is better with a single No. 8 at the top of the loop. Strike (or lift) at any movements.

On the face of it, this approach flies in the face of much of the conventional thinking on pole rigs, where the use of tiny droppers is obligatory and hooks are tied carefully with the line on the inside of the spade. Yet many top anglers have tried the rig and found that it works. It needs a leap of faith, careful plumbing and feeding, and the confidence to persevere with it. Like any rig, it is far from infallible but when it does work it can outfish more conventional rigs. Giles Cochrane's thinking is that the F1s suck the hook (and bait) into their mouths, helped by the fact that the hook can pivot much more freely. The shot so close to the hook helps bite registration. Try it!

Roach

Feeding Habits

In comparison with carp, roach are timid feeders, content to up-end and peck at food on the bottom, or to take bait falling through the water. They will feed in a wider temperature range than will carp: from a heatwave, with water temperatures close to 80 degrees Fahrenheit (26 degrees Celsius), to very cold weather, when the carp are almost dormant.

Roach are very much a shoal fish, and these shoals are grouped by size, although it is common for shoals of different-sized roach to group together. Whilst a water with lots of small roach might see them evenly distributed, a water with a mixture of sizes of roach will result in the bigger roach only being in isolated areas. To catch the better roach you must seek them out, rather than simply fishing at random, and, as the pole angler is seeking roach within pole range, the swim possibilities are further restricted. That is not entirely a bad thing as roach, even big ones,

can often be found close to the bank. If you are to catch them close in it is vital not to scare them, so watch those heavy footfalls. Big roach often follow a short patrol route at regular intervals. With patience it is possible to get them to feed confidently, but if disturbed they will quickly back off from your swim. Swims that have near-side cover, such as reeds, lilies or weedbeds, are easier to fish for roach, as you can take advantage of this cover. It is also much easier to overfeed roach than it is to overfeed other species, so the adage 'little and often' is about right for them.

So how do you find the bigger roach in a water? Spotting the fish is sometimes an option but it is often a case of getting to know a water through trial and error. You need to try different swims and methods and find out about others'

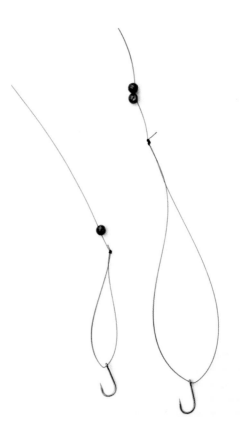

The two basic variants of the hook-in-loop rig: a 2in loop with two No. 8 shot or a 1in loop with one No. 8 shot. The dark line is used for clarity.

121

catches. If matches are held on the water make a note where the bigger roach are usually caught.

Roach in Summer

After the roach spawn in May, it is often difficult to find them for some weeks; they may be in poor condition and reluctant to feed, and it may not be until July that fishing for roach becomes worthwhile again.

Once the roach are feeding in earnest again it is possible to catch them by fishing shallow, using casters as bait. Tackle should be finer than for carp; main line of 0.12 with 0.10 hook link should ordinarily be fine enough. Big roach belt off when hooked, especially when catching shallow and it is

advantageous to use a soft elastic set through a top two kit. This run is usually only 10–12ft rather than right across the lake but try to stop it and the hook is likely to pull out. Choose your elastic depending on the size of fish expected: for fish up to a pound, size 4 is adequate, but if you expect bigger fish, step up to size 6.

One well-proven rig for fishing up in the water uses a small float with a bulk of just three No. 10 or No. 11 shot set just below halfway from the hook to the float. No dropper shot is used. This is used with casters fishing very shallow with a short line and the roach hook themselves against the elastic. Try a fine-wire size 16 hook if they will have it; otherwise, scale down

By fishing up in the water with casters Mark caught a succession of good-sized roach, including this 8oz sample.

The up-in-the-water roach rig.

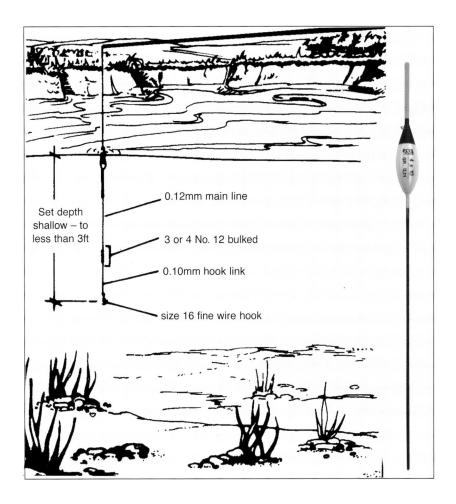

Set depth shallow – to less than 3ft

0.12mm main line

3 or 4 No. 12 bulked

0.10mm hook link

size 16 fine wire hook

to a size 18 or 20. Another tip is to try just the half-inch tip of a worm instead of caster as hook bait. You can continue to feed casters but you may find the piece of worm is a more robust hook bait. With both casters and the worm head, just nick the bait on the hook so that the hook point is showing.

In shallow water less than about 6ft deep, this up-in-the-water approach can be combined with a full-depth rig. Set up another top with a float taking around 0.4g and a small bulk plus droppers set to fish on the bottom. The casters that the surface-feeding fish miss will attract more fish that are content to bottom-feed. Other fish, such as bream, crucians and tench, may also turn up. It may be more prudent to set up this bottom rig with size 6 elastic.

Roach in Winter

Winter roach fishing is more straightforward. Location is the key to success as the roach can be shoaled in some areas of a lake and entirely absent from others. Finesse is important so a main line of 0.10mm with hook links of 0.09 or 0.08 should be matched with fine elastic – No. 4 is a good starting point.

Float choice is dictated by depth and conditions – 0.1g per foot of depth is an excellent starting point, and a float with a fine bristle will aid bite detection. Shot the float with a small bulk set at least 2ft from the hook with two or three tiny dropper shot. In shallow water of less than 4ft it may be better to dispense with the bulk and simply use a shotting pattern of strung out small shot.

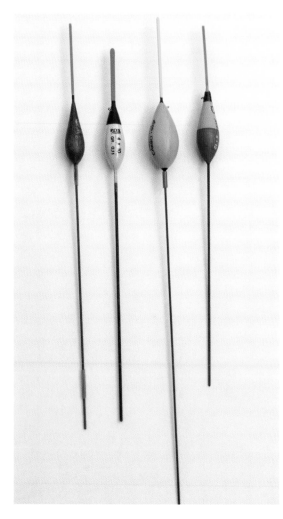

Typical pole floats for roach fishing, which are ideal for the added finesse that it demands.

Provided the water is not overrun with tiny roach, it is a case of building the swim patiently. The better fish may take some time to appear, so do not be too impatient. If there are high numbers of tiny roach that keep taking the bait, try casters as hook bait, feeding a mixture of hemp and caster. In both cases keep the hook small and fine wire; a size 20 is ideal but you may need to go down to a size 22.

As an alternative bait presentation try a very light rig with just one No. 10 shot per foot of depth, with the shot spread out. Very regular feeding will encourage the roach to take on the drop, and the pole is ideal for this delicate form of presentation. Lay the rig on the water to get a slow drop.

Sometimes this method can result in lots of fast, unhittable bites. To slow them down, change to feeding one big handful of bait every twenty or thirty minutes, feeding nothing in between. The roach should stop dashing around and feed in a more leisurely fashion on the bottom. Try laying the bait (especially casters) over depth on the bottom. With casters, try burying the hook inside the caster, taking care not to burst it.

Bream in Stillwaters

Bream fishing on the pole is similar to roach fishing except that bream do not fight particularly hard, even though you may be catching them weighing considerably more than the average roach. Certainly, you could consider increasing the strength of the tackle slightly and the elastic to match it, but, generally, tackle matched to elastic in the range 6 to 8 is adequate. Bream feed mostly on the bottom, although in summer they can feed at mid-depth or even near the surface, perhaps 2–3ft down. Bream are often found in deeper water than carp; *see* Chapter 7 for the ideal methods.

Traditionally, bream are caught on baits such as maggots, casters, bread and worms, but the widespread increase in the use of pellets and fishmeal has changed thinking about this. It is now common to catch them on soft pellets over

Although there are many bait alternatives for catching roach in winter, caster, pinkies, bloodworm and maggots are all possibilities. Maggots are the simplest and most reliable, in all but the most difficult of conditions, and roach have a preference for bronze maggots. Ensure that you carefully clean the maggots with maize meal before use.

Feed the swim little and often. Little can be as few as two or three maggots, although more than this is usually acceptable. What you should generally avoid is throwing in great handfuls of bait.

Use pole rests to hold the pole to give a target to aim at when groundbaiting for bream.

fishmeal groundbaits, and they also like sweet-corn and luncheon meat. When bream are feeding well it can take a large quantity of bait to hold a big shoal. What that bait is depends on the water; casters and pellets are highly rated for getting a shoal of bream foraging hard.

Catching Big Fish from Stillwaters

There is a great deal of difference between the pole angler's approach and that of the dedicated big fish angler. It is not possible for the pole angler to emulate the long casting tactics of the typical carp angler, nor the long fishing sessions with several rods. He can only fish at close range, and yet can successfully target and land good-sized fish. Although it is possible to land carp to double figures, and sometimes weighing more than 20lb, pole fishing is not suited to targeting big carp. However, there is no reason why the pole angler should not catch big fish of other species such as roach, perch, crucians, ide, bream and rudd.

Medium-sized bream are an ideal target for the pole angler fishing gravel pits.

Tench of a good size can also be caught, although the big ones are far more likely to be found in a large gravel pit or lake than in a small commercial fishery, and, tactically, fishing with a pole on such waters is limiting. Nevertheless, quality tench to 8lb are caught on the pole every year. Both male and female tench scrap very hard, but certainly the hardest fighter is the male, with his big paddle-shaped pelvic fins. A bristling 4lb male tench can easily fool an angler into thinking he is connected to a double-figure carp.

Pole fishing offers a way to present a bait with a precision unmatched by any other method, and the pole angler can also feed a swim with great accuracy. Furthermore, fishing with a pole can sometimes offer advantages in playing a fish,

A big crucian – this 2lb-plus specimen was caught by Mark – is an ideal big-fish target for the pole angler.

so fishing with a pole should not be discounted as a method for catching big fish. Where the pole angler can score with big fish is when fishing those sneaky swims where big fish like to hide. Stealth is essential, as is careful feeding.

Is There a Secret to Finding the Big Fish?

When it comes to finding the bigger fish in a water there are several important things to consider. For one thing, big fish are not distributed evenly throughout a water like currants in a cake. There are fewer of them than their smaller brethren. They favour spots that give them an instinctive sense of security, yet are not too far from a reliable feeding area. That means there could be underwater features, snags or weed-beds close by. Their feeding areas may be frequented only at certain times of the day, or they may be prepared to feed confidently only when conditions are right – this might mean when it is cloudy, or windy, or when there is some colour in the water.

There are several ways to locate the fish you seek: trial and error through fishing; asking other anglers, the fishery owner or bailiff for advice; spending time learning about the water by plumbing it to discover the underwater contours, and employing observation and experience to try to discover the likeliest spots. Most likely you will need to use a combination of all three methods to get a feel for the water. Whatever you do, try not to fall into the common trap of simply going to the most popular spot on the lake, which is often the one closest to the car park.

Larger, 'natural', gravel-pit-type waters are more likely to produce big fish than small, heavily stocked commercial fisheries. With one particular exception: there are some small waters that have some very big fish, either through excellent fishery management, or simply because the water is very productive and well suited to at least one species growing to a good size. Big perch can sometimes be found in small waters that have a high number of small fish as prey food. However, the more natural waters, especially fertile mature pits with low stocking densities, give many species a chance to grow fast and large. Location is more difficult than on the much smaller waters, and the pole angler needs to find the fish within pole range, yet gravel pits that have matured over twenty years or more often have plenty of overhanging willows that offer sanctuary to big fish. Their depths may also vary a great deal, as will the composition of the bottom – from soft silt and mud to hard gravel and sand. It may take much more effort to get to know larger waters well, but in the long run the rewards may far exceed those offered by an easier, more predictable water.

Having found the swim, choose your tactics carefully. Remember you are targeting big fish, not – as the late and great match angler Ivan Marks once put it – just fishing for bites. Think about how you want to feed the swim, what bait to use on the hook and what tackle to use. Consider the habits of the particular species. Whereas when you started pole fishing you might have been glad to catch any fish, now you want to avoid the tiddlers, and even the medium-sized fish. Consider using bigger baits on bigger hooks: double sweetcorn, paste, big pellets, a large cube of meat, or a lobworm.

Ask yourself the following questions:

- Which species am I targeting?
- Do I need to step up my tackle to play the fish successfully?
- How will I present my bait; are there snags to contend with?
- Am I able to get comfortable in the swim while not scaring all the fish?
- Is it possible to manoeuvre the pole and land hooked fish successfully?
- Are there certain conditions in which the bigger fish are likely to be present and feeding?

Find the answers and there is no reason why you should not catch big fish on the pole.

9 POLE FISHING ON RIVERS

The Basics

Pole fishing a river requires a variety of float-fishing methods, and it will take time to acquire the skills needed to master these methods due to the river currents. Fishing a very slow river with a pole is little more difficult than fishing a stillwater but, when the flow increases slightly, the technique becomes more challenging. The traditional way of float fishing a river is by trotting a float – casting in and allowing the float, under control, to travel down the river. Refined, this technique is highly successful. With careful feeding of the swim and good float control it is possible to attract fish into the swim and explore the water, in both cases taking advantage of the current.

A conventional rod and reel makes it easy to pay line off the reel to the float and search the swim. The pole angler is not able to trot the swim in this way, but, by adjusting the rig, feeding the swim to concentrate the fish within pole range, and extending the pole during the trot, pole fishing on a river is a deadly method. On slower rivers it can easily outfish conventional trotting tactics. The improvements in bait presentation, bite detection, and even speed of fishing are tremendous.

Although your final catch may be less than on a heavily stocked commercial fishery, a fine autumn day's pole fishing on a river like the Thames can be equally satisfying.

This fine dace of 8oz is a worthy quarry for the river pole angler. The float shown is ideal for medium-paced rivers.

It is possible to pole fish the first half of a typical 20-yard river trotting swim successfully at a range of up to 10m from the bank; the shorter the trot, the longer the possible range from the bank. The aim is to create a killing zone in the first 15ft of the trot, and the way you feed the swim is the vital ingredient to success, for you need to attract the fish to within pole trotting range. It is also important to prevent the fish from feeding upstream of your fishing spot, which is almost always a consequence of feeding too far upstream.

Reading the Swim

It is more important to read the swim on a river than on a stillwater. On a stillwater you have to understand the underwater depths and contours, but on a river it is essential to take the currents and weedbeds into account, too. You must find the likely holding spots of the fish within the swim. Doing that is the tricky part. No two rivers are identical, swims vary enormously even in the same river, and different species favour various parts of the river.

Totally slack water rarely holds many fish on rivers with some flow, except in times of flood. It is more likely that you will find the fish in the flow, especially roach, dace and chub. Weedbeds attract fish on rivers, especially big roach, which like to browse among underwater lily beds (commonly called 'cabbages'). If there is clean gravel beyond such a 'cabbage patch', perhaps with floating lilies close in, then it is potentially a

A river swim will offer several possibilities for the pole angler, with varying current speeds and even the chance of a run close to the island. This swim holds roach, dace, perch and chub.

roach swim. Perch prefer deeper holes near those dark green bulrushes also known as 'pipe reeds'; do not confuse these with great reed-mace, which have thick brown tops. Dace shoal on shallow gravelly glides in summer and in winter form huge shoals prior to spawning. Chub keep well away from disturbance, which is why you will often achieve success fishing to far-bank cover such as bushes trailing in the water. A quiet approach and some nearside cover, especially when fishing outside of the disturbance of match conditions, may give you a chance of catching them on a pole. Bream seem to turn up just about anywhere and it is often a case of knowing their haunts.

All this presumes 'normal' conditions. In high- or low-water conditions, the fish may behave differently. With extra water, 'dead' water may become productive as fish shelter out of the main current. In drought conditions, the fish seek more oxygenated water, which is faster than normal or lies near to weedbeds.

No river is truly uniform and bends push the current to the outside of the bend, leaving slower water on the inside. This gives the angler the chance to choose his swim according to conditions. Changes in depth speed up or slow down the current, and a truly wild river shows this pattern of pools and shallows at its best. Even in canalized rivers, winter floods alter the contours of the river, giving it some character. On rivers the surface water is usually flowing faster than the water near the river bed, owing to the irregularities near the bed. This means that slowing the progress of the float is vital, to match the slower progress of the loose feed as it gets near the bottom.

The water colour usually varies according to the conditions. A river where the level is reducing – 'fining down', as it is commonly known – and carrying a tinge of colour may prove ideal for many species. Very clear or heavily coloured water often provide the trickiest of conditions. Water clarity may determine the tactical approach, with clear water demanding much finer tackle than coloured water.

Equipment

Pole fishing on rivers is a much more active form of pole fishing than it is on stillwaters. The target species are generally smaller, fish up to 2 or 3lb perhaps, so for general work it is better to tackle river pole fishing with a lightweight match pole. A stronger all-round pole or power pole is more suitable when targeting bigger fish with a static bait.

Consider the ideal action for a river pole. For fishing a short line, a light, stiff pole is ideal. (A 'short' line on rivers is different from that on stillwaters, meaning around 3–8ft.) For long-line pole fishing on rivers with the rig set up to fish from 6–10m to hand it is easier to use a pole with some flex. A viable alternative for fishing to hand is to use a system whip of 5–9m, providing the target fish are less than 8oz.

Early attempts to pole fish on rivers saw anglers using conventional stick floats with a pole. It ought to work but the drag in a rod and reel set-up makes the float behave differently from the way it does when used with a pole. The availability of much better floats for river pole fishing changed this, making it unnecessary to use conventional floats.

Initially, keep pole floats for river fishing simple. Bodied floats taking from 0.5g to 2g are a good starting point. Ensure that they have bristles around 1 to 2mm and carbon-fibre stems. To begin with, use standard split shot to form bulk shot loads but as you gain river experience you will find tungsten olivettes more useful.

Basic Trotting with a Pole

Choose a Suitable Swim

For your initial attempts at pole fishing a river, swim choice is paramount. You are unlikely to find a sturdy platform as river banks are usually uneven and much wilder than man-made ones.

Try to find a river swim with the following characteristics:

- A flat and low bank.
- An even depth (5–7ft) and steady flow. Avoid flows faster than around a foot per second. It is easier to start on steady, slower-paced water.
- A clear trot, unhindered by weed. It may be that there is a clear run-through on one line but not another.
- Plenty of small fish such as dace, roach and perch present.
- A sheltered spot, preferably away from boat traffic and other disturbances.
- Calm conditions.

Bait

You will need the right bait for the water and a good starting point is two pints of maggots. On some rivers in summer, maggots can be so attractive to tiddlers such as bleak that casters (with some hemp to mix in as feed) may prove better. Get advice from local anglers and tackle dealers who know the stretch.

Bait choices on rivers are fewer than they are on stillwaters. Almost all river pole fishing can

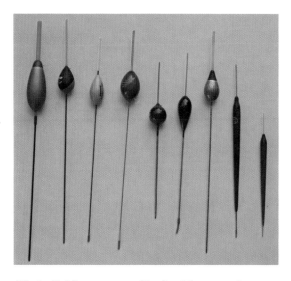

The bodied floats are capable of tackling most river pole fishing. The slim floats (right) are ideal for hemp fishing.

The basic river rig: a bulk plus droppers.

long line to pole

0.12mm main line

FLOW

olivette

No. 8

2 × No. 10 droppers

be achieved with one or more of the following: maggots, casters, hemp, tares, sweetcorn, worms and bread, plus groundbaits.

Getting Started

When trotting a river with rod and line, it is easier to go about it standing up, but it is easier to pole fish sitting down. Get your box positioned level, with a well-supported foot plate. Assuming you find the ideal depth of 5–7ft, set up the pole at just 6m with a rig taking around 1g. Plumb the depth carefully using a heavy plummet,

checking the depth both further out from the bank and down the swim. Look for a swim that is even in depth and has a clear run that is free from weed. Bulk nearly all the shot load around 2ft from the hook with two or three No. 10 droppers below this at 6- to 8in intervals. Shot the float well down with half an inch of bristle showing. Set the initial depth slightly deeper than the plumbed depth. The slower the water, the nearer the actual depth you should set the float. This set-up has around 15ft of line above the float, giving a reasonable length of trot. Set

Fishing 7m or so of pole to hand is the simplest way to tackle river pole fishing. The pole holder, known as a tulip (an alternative to a pole sock), is used to hold spare pole sections.

up the rig with 0.12mm line with a size 20 hook to 0.10mm line as a starting point. Match this to either size 4, 5 or 6 elastic. A rule of thumb is that the heavier the rig the more likely the need for heavier elastic.

The fishing itself is simple enough. Swing the rig out gently underhand, taking care that the rig does not land in a heap. Control the line with the pole so that the line is upstream of the float. Keep the pole in touch with the float so that with a little control it is possible to slow the progress of the float through the swim. If the float rides up out of the water add another small shot, say, a No. 8, to the bulk. Finely tune this balance of holding the float back and over-shotting to achieve good bait presentation.

Feeding

Regular feeding is vital on a river. Every cast, throw fifteen to twenty maggots straight out in front of you on the line of the trot. The river current will carry these downstream, attracting fish upstream to the swim. You need to give careful consideration to the quantity and frequency of feeding the swim. If you overfeed, the fish will tend to drop back out of the swim; if you underfeed, the fish may come right to the head of the swim, or in extreme cases simply disperse, as there is not enough bait going in to hold them.

From here on, it is a case of fishing and experimenting. You may find that you are catching lots of gudgeon on the bottom. If so, try shallowing up a little to see if there are better fish above the gudgeon. It takes time to build a river swim; indeed, it is better that it should be that way. With an instant response it is all too easy to get a quick flurry of fish, then nothing, as the disturbance of catching fish that were never really feeding well unsettles the shoal. Be patient, as with most species the better ones take time to start feeding confidently.

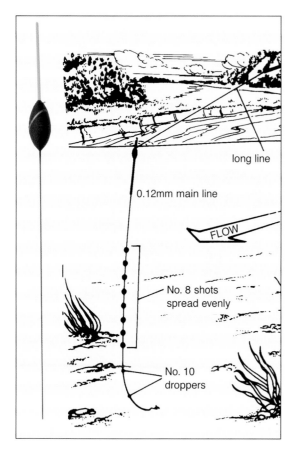

long line

0.12mm main line

FLOW

No. 8 shots
spread evenly

No. 10
droppers

*The alternative river rig: a strung-out
shotting pattern.*

Simple Variations on the Rig

Simple long-line fishing can be very effective on
rivers. As you increase the length of pole, the
trotting and casting range increase too, and the
pole is usable in water with a depth from as little as 3ft to as much as 14ft. In expert hands it
is one of the fastest methods of fishing there is,
and many top river match anglers use it to great
advantage. With different depths and current
speeds there is a need to use different-sized floats.
Increased depth and flow demand greater weight
loads, and on rivers tungsten olivettes are vital.
Their reduced size (tungsten is an extremely
dense and heavy metal) reduces drag and improves presentation.

The simplest variation on the shotting is to
change to a pattern of small shot strung out on
the line at regular intervals. Try using No. 8 shot
and string them out at 6in intervals, with the
shot nearest the hook being a No. 10. This last
shot is the tell-tale shot and is usually 9–12in
from the hook. This rig can give a slow fall to
the bait and a more delicate bait presentation.

As with any shotting pattern, this is merely a
starting point. There are many possibilities, including using different-sized shot, forming the
shot into small bulks, and altering the spacing of
the shot. Whatever you do, try to use small shot,
except in the most rugged of conditions; in this
way you can take advantage of the delicacy offered by the pole method. With practice you will
know when the float is going through the swim
correctly, and your results will reflect this.

Long-Pole/Short-Line on Rivers

With the pole-to-hand method there is necessarily a long length of line above the float. This is
not always desirable, and to get the best out of
pole fishing on a river it is essential to master the
long-pole/short-line technique. This is broadly
similar to the technique used on stillwaters (*see*
page 97), with the rider that trotting the float demands a longer line above the float.

The level-banked, even-paced, even-depth
swim, holding plenty of fish, is ideal. Begin by
fishing at a modest range, perhaps using 8m of
pole. This means that the rig (start with the
bulked rig) will be set up to match the pole at
4m, so that with the float around 5–6ft deep
there is around 8ft of line above the float. To
fish the swim you will be adding either two or
three joints. This does not give you a particularly long trot, yet, with accurate feeding, carefully judged to hit bottom within the confines of
the trot, the fish should respond.

The difference is that you now have much
closer control over the float. You can slow the
float with great precision and hit bites more easily. As the float reaches the end of the limited
trot you can carefully add joints one at a time to

increase the trot. You may want to reduce further the length of line above the float.

Experiment with over-shotting the float. It is best if the swim has some flow for this, as you are trying to get a balance between the controlled retarding of the line with the pole and the sinking effect of the extra shot on the float. With care it is possible to slow the float a great deal in the flow. You will need to increase the depth slightly to counteract the effect of the flow lifting the bait from the bottom. This method takes much practice and it is vital to match the float and shotting to the flow. Once you have mastered it at ever greater lengths of pole, you will have a method that can prove superior to conventional rod and reel technique.

Mark used this method to great effect on an autumn Upper Thames match one year. The river was in perfect condition, with a tinge of colour and steady flow, yet stick float tactics produced only a handful of small roach. A switch to pole tactics, using a 0.5g float, slightly over-shotted, fished at 9m, produced a succession of quality roach on bronze maggot on a 22 hook. The final bag included roach over a pound, and at 13lb was enough to take second place, while the anglers fishing conventionally on either side failed to break a pound.

Advanced Feeding Techniques on Running Water

Getting Feed Down Quickly
Introducing loose feed either by hand or catapult is not always enough to concentrate the fish within pole trotting range. The bait needs to get down to the river bed more quickly. Maggots, casters and hemp all sink slowly through the water, maggots being slowest of all at about eight

Accurate groundbaiting can concentrate the fish in a river swim.

Groundbaits that bind well yet break up in a controlled manner, and can hold plenty of added feed such as casters, are ideal for river pole fishing.

seconds per foot, and hemp quickest at six seconds per foot; casters are in between. In a deep, pacy swim, the maggots will be well downstream before they hit bottom. If the current is 2ft per second and the swim is 10ft deep, even allowing for slowing of the current near the bottom the maggots will be nearly 20ft down the swim before hitting bottom.

There are two methods of getting feed down more quickly: using groundbait, or using a bait dropper. Modern groundbaits are fish attractants in their own right, and break up in a controlled manner. River groundbaits should bind well so that the groundbait gets to the bottom without breaking up. In very fast water add a special binder such as PV1, or add molehill soil to make the groundbait heavier. Add bait samples to the groundbait; casters and hemp are good, but you need to take more care with maggots as too many will split the groundbait ball.

Groundbait on Rivers

One effective groundbaiting technique on rivers is to ball it in when you start fishing. Once you have plumbed the swim and checked that you

have a clear run through without snagging up, place the pole in pole rests. Mix the groundbait thoroughly, allow it to stand for ten minutes to soak up the water, and re-wet it if necessary. If you throw in groundbait that is too dry, you may find the balls of groundbait floating off downstream before they sink many yards away. Ball up about ten lumps of groundbait (around tennis ball size), and throw them in a tight patch about a yard downstream of the pole tip, rather than in front of you or upstream. The pole works best when you are presenting the bait over the groundbait rather than beyond it. By doing this it is easy to get the rig settled and under close control as it trots on to the baited patch.

This quantity is a starting point, and the amount you use is entirely dependent on how much you are expecting to catch. Sometimes you will need much less, other times much more. If you have judged the quantity correctly, there should be a good response from the fish for two to three hours. Then, assuming the bites have dried up, it is time to try rebaiting, usually with around half the amount of the original baiting.

There is always a risk that this method will not work, which is all part of the fun of fishing. When it does work it can be far better than relying simply on loose feed, concentrating the fish on the groundbaited patch. It takes experience and experimentation to get the best from this method, and it may be possible to loose feed as well. Vary the mix according to conditions: dark, low-feed mixes are best for cold, clear winter fishing; lighter-coloured, high-feed mixes are better in ideal conditions of winter rivers in perfect trim with a tinge of colour, when the fish are likely to be hungry.

Using a Bait Dropper

Bait droppers are ideal for getting bait on the bottom at the head of the swim without using groundbait, especially when using chopped worm for perch and other big fish. The long line used for river pole fishing is a hindrance to using a bait dropper. If you try to ship it out it will drag in the river and open before you can get it into position. To prevent this, fix a cable tie to

Using a bait dropper to place chopped worms, caster, maggots or hemp is an accurate way to feed a river swim.

Use a cable tie to hold the bait dropper against the pole until you have manoeuvred the pole into position. Twist the pole to release the dropper while holding the extended pole high enough for the dropper to clear the water, then lower the dropper into the swim to hit bottom at the release point.

the section of pole just above where the bait dropper reaches. Leave the tag end uncut so that you can hook the line just above the bait dropper on the tag. This allows you to ship the pole out and raise it high enough in the air to ensure the dropper is clear of the water when you rotate the pole to free the dropper. Then you can lower the dropper into the water where you want it – around a yard downstream is ideal.

Presenting a Still or Slow-Moving Bait

Using a Lollipop Float

Having laid a carpet of bait on the bottom, it is advantageous to fish either a still or very slow-moving bait on top of it. In moderate flows this can be accomplished using conventional pole floats, although you will need to increase the size of float, slightly overload it and increase the rig depth. The alternative is to use a lollipop float, which allows a reduced shot load in modest flows and gives you the ability to present a still bait in more powerful flows. These floats, with their disc bodies, present the slim edge to the current and, with the bristle angled to the body, provide almost perfect, still bait presentation. It is vital to choose a float of the right size, get it shotted right, and hold the pole still when fishing it. When you have the right size float the bristle is vertical in the water: if it is angled towards the pole, it is too light; if angled away, it is too heavy. Some lollipop floats are attached simply with silicon rubbers and, in conjunction with

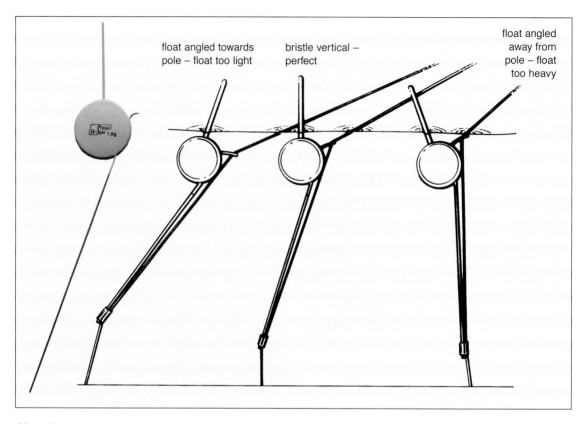

float angled towards
pole – float too light

bristle vertical –
perfect

float angled
away from
pole – float
too heavy

If you have a flat float of the right size, the bristle should be vertical.

olivettes attached by rubbers, can be changed until the right size float is found.

Carefully adjust the shot load and depth to get the presentation just right. Set the bulk shot or olivette so that it is just off bottom, with two small dropper shot (No. 8 or No. 10) spaced out below this. Set the bulk about 18in from the hook so that the rig is about 15in over depth. Err on the heavy side for your main line – 0.16 or 0.18mm is about right – and change the elastic to a heavier grade than usual to allow for the extra resistance to the strike. To fish a section of lobworm on the bottom – a deadly method that accounts for many big perch, tench, bream, chub and even barbel (not forgetting big eels) – you will need to use a strong size 14 or 12 hook (Kamasan B711 is ideal) tied to 0.14 or 0.16mm line. This style of fishing is targeting big fish, far removed from delicate roach fishing, and there-

fore size 8 elastic is a minimum. Consider using size 10 or 12, or even 14 if necessary. Increase the size of the dropper shots too.

Using these floats enables you to present either a completely still bait or a bait that you can just inch through, and this applies to water that is barely moving as well as water that moves with pace. Use a spray bar to hold the pole completely still.

The Pole Feeder Method

There is another way to present a still bait in strong-flowing rivers. Lowestoft angler Nick Larkin has spent years perfecting a method to tackle the bream and big roach in the tidal Norfolk rivers Yare and Wensum. Faced with powerful flows and deep water he looked for a way to combine pole fishing with the use of a swimfeeder. The advantage of such a method is pinpoint feeding, despite the strong flows, combined with sensitive bite registration.

The end tackle is simplicity itself. A short 2in link with link swivel for the feeder is combined with a 20in hook link, which may have a shot near the hook to help pin down the bait. Use a main line of 0.16mm and 0.12mm for hook links. Nick Larkin favours his own-brand NISA swimfeeders, which have the weight concentrated in the base rather than on the side, to get the feeder to remain upright. Conventional open-end and block-end feeders should do the job adequately.

Bite detection has proved the hardest challenge over the years. Initial attempts with elastic running through quiver-tip-type pole tops proved cumbersome and prone to tangling. The latest and best method is to use a pole rigged conventionally with No. 12 elastic and a Stonfo. Take a 12in length of fine elastic (1, 2 or 3) and form a small loop in one end – this will be attached with the rig to the hook on the Stonfo. At the other end of the elastic you need a means of fastening the elastic to the rig line so that there is a loop of slack line in the rig. The fine elastic then shows the bite by stretching within the confines of the slack line, and the bite is also shown on a bite indicator.

For an adjustable method, you can drill a conventional leger stop peg with a bait drill and thread the end of the elastic through the peg and stop it by tying on a bead. The tube of the leger stop must be threaded on the rig and then the peg used to secure the elastic with the slack loop of rig line. For a fixed method, introduce a swivel or large rig ring into the pole rig a foot or so from the conventional loop and knot the fine elastic to this to give a slack loop.

Whichever method you use, it is vital to hold the pole still, and a bump or spray bar will make this much easier. You may need to experiment with different strengths and lengths of fine elastic and the amount of slack line in the rig.

This method is for targeting big fish, so use baits such as double maggot, caster or a redworm on a size 16 or 14 hook. Use a heavy, rich mix in the feeder, laced with chopped worm and casters. It is very much a method that requires

A specially designed feeder with weight at the bottom so that it sits upright on the river bed.

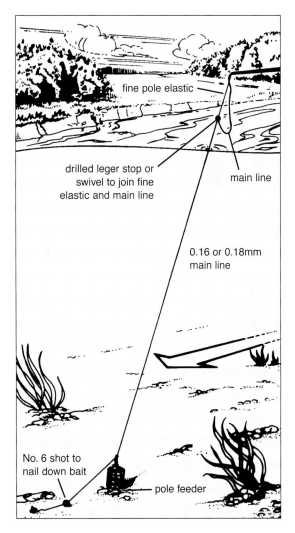

fine pole elastic

drilled leger stop or swivel to join fine elastic and main line

main line

0.16 or 0.18mm main line

No. 6 shot to nail down bait

pole feeder

The pole feeder rig.

patience and concentration, as it may be two or three hours before the big fish show.

River Pole Methods for Roach

Hemp Fishing

Fishing with hempseed for roach is a method that is long established. Its selectiveness makes it ideal in avoiding the tiddlers that often abound in summer, and fished with skill it can account for good bags of quality roach. To get the best out of hemp fishing for roach it is vital to understand that a delicate approach will make a big difference to your results. Fishing hemp with a pole takes advantage of the delicate bait pre-

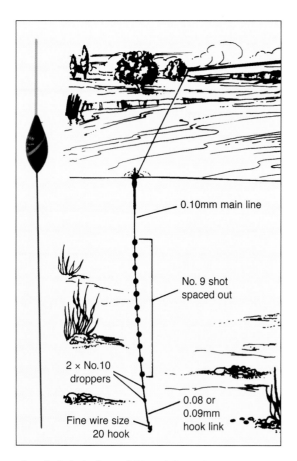

0.10mm main line

No. 9 shot
spaced out

2 × No.10
droppers

Fine wire size
20 hook

0.08 or
0.09mm
hook link

A typical rig for hemp fishing; delicacy is paramount here.

sentation and bite detection the pole offers, and in many circumstances fishing hemp this way is far superior to attempting to fish hemp with a rod and reel. One of the bugbears of hemp fishing has always been 'unhittable' bites; sometimes you may fail to hit nine bites in ten! Fortunately, the right rigs and correct feeding can largely overcome this.

The method works in waters with a decent head of roach, and is a noted method on the Nene, Warwickshire Avon and Thames, as well as on many other rivers. In late summer the roach shoal up and it is just a matter of finding them. Roach are creatures of habit and these areas vary little from year to year. Once you know the hotspots you can return to them year after year, with the roach fishing coming into its best in late summer. Hedge your bets on waters that are not fed with hemp by fishing it in conjunction with casters. That way you can use casters as bait while feeding hemp, and periodically try hemp on the hook.

Summer hemp fishing is all about finesse. This means light elastics such as size 4, a 0.10mm main line, and hook links of 0.08mm coupled with fine-wire hooks. The Kamasan B511 in size 20 and 18 is ideal. An ideal float rig for hemp is to use a small slim float with a shot load equating to around 0.1g per foot of depth. Shot this with small shot such as No. 8s and 10s, and spread the shot out to get a slow fall to the bait, which is useful if the roach come off the bottom to intercept the loose-fed hemp.

For your hemp fishing you will need at least a pint of fresh hemp, either cooked yourself from dry or bought as a can of ready-cooked. Giant hemp is the best for hook bait, and it is vital that the split in the grains when cooked is just enough to insert the bend of the hook. Overcooked, it is OK for feed but nearly impossible to put on the hook.

There are two schools of thought regarding feeding when hemp fishing. The traditional one is to feed very small amounts – just a few grains – regularly. This method works but the alternative, which is to start by feeding a good bed of hemp (three or four big handfuls), then feeding little

Hook hemp by inserting the bend of a fine-wire hook into the split of the seed.

and often, can work even better. The bed of hemp creates a hemp oil slick that attracts the roach far better than just the drip of a few grains.

Roach may take hemp from the start, but it is more usual for it to take two or three hours to work. Expert hemp anglers fish another line, only periodically trying the hemp line, until they are sure that the roach are taking the hemp confidently. Set the hemp rig to fish the exact depth, at least initially, and be prepared to shallow up or change rigs to a lighter one. Bites should be confident and easy to hit. If you get lots of fast, unhittable bites, you should try feeding more heavily but much less regularly. This forces the roach to stop competing so madly, and slows down their feeding.

Alternative hook baits for hemp include tares (a small brown pea), maple peas (a large brown pea) and elderberries in season. These baits are all larger than hemp and you should scale up the hook size while retaining a fine-wire pattern.

Bread Punch Fishing

Using a pole to present bread punch to catch large numbers of roach on rivers is a deadly winter method. There are at least two effective approaches. The first one is a winter method used in clear water on slow Fenland waters such as the Old Nene, when conditions are clear. Top anglers such as Bob Nudd have perfected this

in match conditions to catch up to 500 roach in five hours. The second variation is an all-season method (although it is at its best in perfect winter conditions), which works on a wide variety of waters, including the Bristol Avon, Dorset Stour, and Thames.

The Fenland Approach

Speed is of the essence to catch large numbers of small roach in a match, and this method takes short cuts in its quest for speed. Wherever possible, try to get set up to fish the pole to hand, at 5 or 6m if possible. To make the float rig easy to control, use a slim, pear-shaped float taking at least 0.75g (an olivette as bulk about 2ft from the hook) with two or three tiny droppers. This weight gets the bait down to the fish quickly. Use a 0.10mm main line with hook links of 0.08mm. As the main target fish are small roach use a small bread punch; the ideal hook is the Kamasan B511, size 20. Plumb the depth carefully and start off with the hook set about an inch off bottom. As the session progresses, experiment by trying it shallower.

Correct feeding is vital to success. For this method use special punch crumb. This groundbait is tricky to mix up, and many experienced anglers mix it the night before fishing. Add small quantities of water to the bread. Allow the groundbait to stand for a while, absorbing the water, then add more water until it is a perfect fluffy mix. If you get it wrong, a useless stodge will be the result. To eradicate lumps, push the mix through a fine riddle. An alternative groundbait is liquidized bread.

For speed it is best to feed by hand, gently squeezing small balls of the crumb, which vary from walnut to golf-ball size. This groundbait sinks slowly. In very gentle currents, this does not matter but in slightly faster water there is a way around this. Sieve some aquarium gravel to retain the smallest (3–4mm) stones. Mix the gravel in with the crumb and the crumb will go down much quicker. Feed regularly, judging the amount and regularity to the expected catch. On a cold, clear canal that could mean a tiny thumbnail-sized ball every twenty minutes; on a

Punch crumb can be tricky to mix, but using a water spray makes it easier to achieve the correct fluffy texture.

Home-made bread punches are ideal for tackling big roach using punched bread on the pole on rivers. The hard balsa handles ensure that they float if dropped and the bright colour makes them easy to locate.

fish-filled river, you might need a golf ball every cast. Only knowledge of the venue, peg and conditions, coupled with practice and experience, will help you to get it right most of the time.

As an added attractant to hold the roach, put down a bed of hemp. There is no doubt that the oil given off will eventually bring in the bigger roach. The best hook bait is medium-sliced long-life white bread, its tackiness making it usable for longer than ordinary bread. There is no need to roll the bread; just keep the unused slices in the wrapper.

The West Country Method

You can use the traditional West Country bread-punch method at any time in the season and in a wide variety of conditions. This is a method for hungry fish, best suited to ideal conditions on a river with a tinge of colour, yet it can work in summer conditions and catch far more than just roach. Bream are an alternative target, and dace and chub can also succumb. Originally developed for rod and line fishing on the Bristol Avon, it can be easily adapted by the pole angler for use anywhere the fish are willing to accept groundbait and bread as bait.

The method is similar to the Fen method. There are two differences. The first is that you use normal groundbait. Plain brown crumb can work well enough, although some of the continental groundbaits such as Sensas Gros Gardons (French for 'big roach') can outscore it. As with the punch-crumb method the feed rate is crucial and relies on understanding the conditions. A good starting point is to introduce a golf-ball-sized ball every ten minutes. The second difference is that the punch used is much bigger, usually a size 16, but no smaller than a size 18. That means the strength of the rig needs to be stepped up to at least 0.12mm main line and 0.10mm hook link. Again, use fine-wire hooks.

10 POLE FISHING ON CANALS

Kevin Ashurst once compared canal fishing to the intricacies of a Swiss watch: 'Everything is miniaturized.' On a barge canal there is a limited amount of water to fish, the water is likely to be shallow, the fish are shy and only the finest tackle is likely to succeed. Feeding the swim must be measured and accurate. To the angler used to fishing rivers or modern commercials it can be difficult to adapt to fishing a tough canal. That said, practising the skills needed on a canal is good fun in its own right, and will stand you in good stead elsewhere.

There has been a revolution in canal fishing in the last few years, triggered by two changes. First, there seem to be many more and far bigger fish to catch on a number of canals. Second, with better fish to target, anglers are adapting methods developed on commercial fisheries to use on canals.

There are several hazards to fishing a canal. The most obvious – particularly where some

The Oxford Canal is a typical barge canal with a width around 12m and depths to around 4ft in the centre of the boat channel.

inner-city canals are concerned – is their location. Many are in less than salubrious settings with an all too real danger of encountering some of life's less savoury characters. Traffic is another hazard, with boats passing by and even mooring in front of you. Other users of the towpath can present a danger, especially if you obstruct the path with your pole or gear. The first thing you may hear of the swift approach of a cyclist is a double crunch as one cycle wheel after the other crushes your pole. If it is practical, ship back your pole parallel to the canal bank, not across it, and keep the towpath clear of your other gear.

Pole fishing barge canals may be considered from three angles: traditional fine-line methods; traditional better-fish methods; and converted commercial fishery methods. Let's also have a brief look at fishing larger canal-like waters, including ship canals and drains.

Traditional Fine-Line Canal Fishing

Traditional canal fishing involved catching a few small fish from the local cut. With venues often semi-polluted, fish were scarce and stunted in size. Standard tactics were tiny floats and hooks with small baits, such as a single maggot, pinkie,

tiny pellets of punched bread, or bloodworms. Whilst conventional rod and reel tactics offered a degree of finesse, with hand-made floats of wisps of balsa, cane and peacock quill, it was the pole revolution in the late 1970s that changed canal tactics for ever. With no need to cast, and carbon poles coming on to the scene, it was not long before top canal anglers recognized the potential of vastly improved bait presentation. A little plastic cup attached to the tip of the pole allowed pinpoint accuracy in feeding tiny balls of neat jokers. With the availability of precision-made Italian pole floats, which took just three or four No. 10 shot, the revolution continued apace.

Today's canal angler is spoilt for choice when it comes to suitable gear: top-class poles, superb fine lines and hooks, excellent floats, plus all the gadgets you can dream of, are all readily available. But success in fine-line canal fishing involves far more than possessing the right gear, of course. As ever, location is the vital ingredient.

Understanding the Basic Features of a Canal

Unless they are disused, the boat traffic on barge canals changes the underwater topography of this type of waterway. The wash from the boats creates a deep channel down the middle of the

Typical canal pole gear: tiny hooks, ultra-fine lines, tiny floats – perfect for tempting small canal fish.

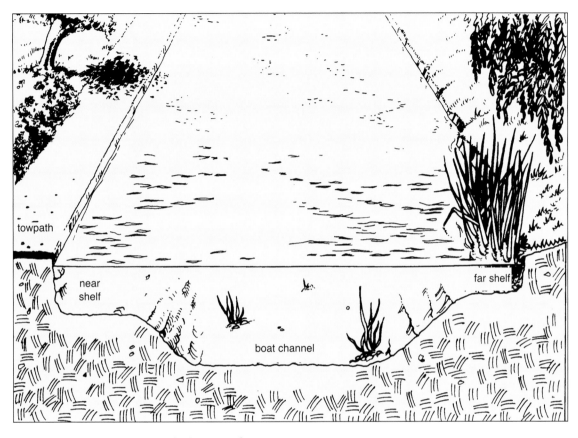

The typical underwater features of a barge canal.

canal, and two shallower areas on each side, known as 'shelves'. Their shape will vary from canal to canal, and they give the angler a clue as to where the fish are most likely to be found. At the base of the near shelf is one probable area. This may not be very far out – possibly even as close as 2m – and may be fishable with a whip.

The base of the far shelf could be as close as 7m but is more likely to be 10–12m away. On the wider parts of canals such as the Grand Union it could be beyond pole reach. Where the far shelf is within reach it offers a likely hotspot, not only at the base of the far shelf but also on the shelf itself, even though it may be much shallower. If it is too shallow – say, less than about 15in – it may be unproductive, and the fish will be found in deeper water nearer the middle. Where there is far-bank cover, for ex-

ample, overhanging branches or rush beds, there is a good chance of big fish being present.

The principal species found in canals are roach, perch, gudgeon, silver bream, bronze bream, chub, and carp. Some canals have flowing pounds and these may also contain dace and bleak.

Excessive boat traffic may make the deeper central channel a lost cause in summer but in winter it may be a viable option. With the two shelves, this gives at least three areas to fish from your peg, which means that careful and accurate plumbing is vital. The experienced canal angler will set up more than one rig with different top sets to cover the various options.

The amount of colour in a canal can very much depend on the time of year. In summer the constant boat traffic churns up the canals and they are often highly coloured. In winter, with hardly any boats moving, the canals are generally much clearer, unless there is a stream feeding in after heavy rain. Many canals have a green algal tinge in winter, offering the ideal conditions for using bread punch.

The precision offered when feeding your swim using a pole pot means it is possible to feed several areas of the swim. On a narrow canal of only around 12m wide it could mean as many as six to eight separate areas. By alternating these areas carefully you can nurse the fishing along so that at no point does the swim die completely.

Basic Rigs

The match angler's small-fish approach on canals revolves around small baits: squatts, pinkies, bloodworm and joker. The pleasure angler can probably get away with normal-sized maggots as well, but these tiny baits demand tiny, fine-wire hooks (sizes 22 to 26) tied to very fine hook links – 0.06 and 0.07mm are the norm, and, even when using maggots or casters, 0.08mm is sufficient. With such fine hook links, main lines can be kept very fine too, with 0.08mm being a good starting point.

Stotz shot are easier to handle than tiny split shot, and vital for minute adjustments on delicate rigs.

The shallowness of the swims, fineness of the tackle and the delicacy of the presentation all point to the use of equally delicate floats. While it is possible to find many small pole floats in common use on commercial fisheries, it is better to use floats specifically designed for canal fishing. These will not only be small, they also have fine bristles and wire stems, so that even the most delicate bites are detectable. These very small floats are marked in Styl weight sizes such as 3×8, 4×10, not to be confused with shot weights! A selection, from 3×8 up to 4×14, will be a good starting point. You will need a selection of the smallest split shot, sizes 8 down to 13, and should consider using both Styl and Stotz weights too.

Fine lines and hooks mean fine elastics fitted to match top sets. Size 2 and 3 elastic is a good starting point for these rigs, and you need only around 18in of it in each tip. For bread punch, a tiny wide gape hook such as a Kamasan B511 in size 22 is ideal. For squatts and pinkies, a fine-wire crystal bend is better, while bloodworm and joker are best tackled with a very fine-wire long-shanked hook.

Shotting these delicate rigs is an art in itself. Depending upon the depth, flow and required presentation there are several options, from a bulk as close to 3in from the hook to catch gudgeon on bloodworm, to rigs with a string of closely spaced No. 13 shot for roach fishing with squatts. The best advice is to use many tiny shot rather than a few bigger shot, and to ensure that the float is dotted right down.

Feeding

Feeding should be sparing but regular. That can mean a few squatts or pinkies, a pinch of jokers held together in some damp leap, or a thumbnail of punch crumb. For the beginner fishing a canal, pinkies are one of the more reliable baits, fished on a size 22 or 24 hook, and you will only need half a pint. Choose the freshest ones you can get. Set the float so that the hook is just tripping bottom. Some canals have a very slight flow, and you will find that using a pole will enable you to control the float carefully, just easing

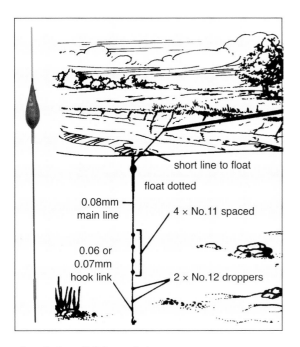

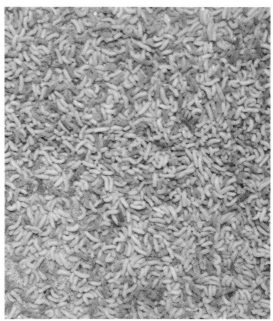

A typical small-fish canal rig.

Pinkies are a useful canal bait for small fish.

it through. With such fine tackle you will need to net anything over a couple of ounces, and take extra care when playing them.

In good summer and autumn conditions, fishing with squatts can be very productive. These tiny maggots are supplied in fine red-brick sand and must be kept damp; failure to do this will result in the squatts drying out, and they will then float. Riddle off the sand before use but periodically spray them with a little water. Feed the swim with squatts with a cata-pult to build a fair-sized area of 4–5ft across. This will give you a variety of spots in which to work and pick off the roach.

Bread-punch fishing is better suited to late autumn and winter, when the water clears. Feed fine punch crumb sparingly and fish the bread punch just off the bottom.

Traditional Better-Fish Methods

One traditional way of exploiting the far side of the canal has been to try to tempt better-sized

Use a small bread punch coupled with fine-wire hooks and fine lines to tempt shy canal roach.

The pole enables the angler to place a rig very close to the far bank with great precision.

roach by laying on with casters. These bigger fish prefer to feed away from the disturbance of the towpath, and by feeding the swim very sparingly for two or three hours it is possible to get the roach feeding confidently before attempting to catch them. There is a greater variety of fish present in canals nowadays, and if there is some cover across the canal within pole reach, such as overhanging bushes, reeds or weedbeds, then bigger fish such as chub and carp may also be present. Ideally, there will be 2ft of water in this far-side area; less than this can make for a struggle as it is all too easy to scare the fish. However, experienced pole anglers have caught from less than a foot of water.

Far-Side Roach
It is vital to understand your target fish – roach, chub or carp? If it is roach, the tactics are simple: fish with a size 3 elastic, a lightweight dibber

rig set over depth, a 0.10mm line and a fine-wire size 20 hook baited with caster. How much you set the rig over depth depends on the draw on the canal but it will usually be at least 6in. Feed sparingly, just half a dozen casters at a time, and completely bury the hook in the caster. Try to leave the far-bank area unfished for at least two hours. When you do fish it, try to catch just a few roach before resting it again for a while. The definition of 'a few' depends very much on the venue: it could be just one or two, or as many as a dozen, but the concept is an important one that applies to other situations in which you are trying to persuade shy fish to settle on your bait.

Canal Chub

Chub demand a step up in tackle strength, and you will need to use stronger hooks, line and elastic, even for modest-sized fish up to a couple of pounds. Your starting point might be 0.14mm main line with 0.12mm hook links with size 6 or 8 elastic in a top two set. Tactically, it may pay to present the bait off the bottom or with a very light on-the-drop rig. When you hook the chub it is vital to ship back quickly to bully it away from the far bank, where it will try to snag you. Play the chub out in mid-canal well away from near- and far-bank snags. Casters are an excellent bait for canal chub but you can step up to offering double caster on a size 18 Drennan Carbon Chub hook.

Canal Carp

Canal carp represent an altogether different proposition. They can be anything from 2 to 20lb, and it is not unusual to get double-figure fish. While there is always a chance of getting a bite from a carp on casters, feeding chopped worm, pellets, sweetcorn and hemp are all likely ways to increase your chances of tempting one. Swims holding carp are often the snaggiest on the entire canal; if there is a substantial area of bushes trailing in the water, there is a good chance of carp being present. Trailing branches mean a high probability of plenty of snags underwater too.

Take a step back and it is easy to see that carp fishing on canals closely resembles margin and island fishing on a commercial fishery. With that thought in mind, tackle carp on a canal in the same way as you would on a stillwater margin swim. Strong pole, strong elastic, strong line and hooks, and a bait to match – this can be the only way to tackle canal carp. There is no point expecting to land a decent-sized carp on 0.10 line when it is likely there will be snags galore. Get that 0.16mm line and size 14 elastic fitted, and attack them. Take advantage of the pole method's accuracy to feed using a pot, and place your rig where it would otherwise be impossible.

For both chub and carp it is worth feeding more than one area of the swim. Always bear in mind that the fish will not necessarily be tight to the far bank, especially if it is very shallow; they may prefer to be where it is at least 18in to 2ft deep.

Mid-Canal Possibilities

Chopped Worm for Perch

It was a big perch revival on the Grand Union Canal that led to the dusting off of the chopped-worm method of old, long before it transferred successfully to commercial venues. Over twenty years ago top canal anglers discovered that in tough, clear winter conditions, using chopped lobworms with a segment of lobworm on the hook would catch big perch (to around 3lb). This method concentrates on the deep mid-canal channel and works wherever there are big perch to be found. Features with deep water are likely perch hotspots. Use strong hooks such as the Kamasan B711 in sizes 14 and 12, with lines to match, and a float with a thick bristle. Fish the worm segment slightly over depth.

Canal Bream in the 'Wides'

Some canals have wide turning bays for the barges, which can be up to 30 yards wide and are often of a good depth. Bream shoals prefer larger areas of the canal and so they often frequent these bays. Tactically, it is usually a case of simple

set rig over depth for base of far shelf

5 × No.8
bulk

0.14mm main line

2 × No.10
droppers bulk

A stillwater float with a thick bristle is ideal for chopped-worm fishing.

*Finely chop worms
with casters to make
an attractive mix.*

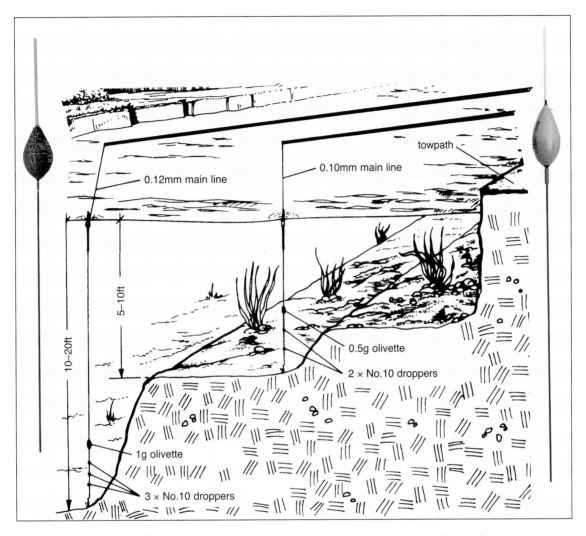

0.12mm main line

0.10mm main line

towpath

5–10ft

10–20ft

0.5g olivette

2 × No.10 droppers

1g olivette

3 × No.10 droppers

You will need two set-ups to cover the nearside shelf and the deep-water channel on deep ship canals.

long-pole fishing out into the centre of the bay, using casters as bait and fishing over depth.

Deep Ship Canals

Ship canals are much deeper and wider than barge canals. Typical examples include those of the Exeter Canal, Gloucester Canal and the Stainforth and Keadby Canal. Depths may reach 20ft in the centre of the canal but more typically these canals are 10–14ft deep within pole range.

As ever, you need to plumb the swim carefully. For roach and perch you are trying to find the bottom of the first shelf, and it may not be that far out – 7–8m of pole is a likely range. Bream tend to be further out, and here you are looking for an area of flat canal bed at a range of 12–14m. The reason for wanting the flat area (which need only be a metre wide) is that groundbaiting is likely to be required to catch bream and skimmers on this type of water. If you groundbait at a point where the bed is steeply sloping, the balls of groundbait will roll away

Graham fishing the Trent and Mersey canal.

from you when they hit the bottom. You will know this because the 'fizz' given off by the groundbait will move away.

For roach and perch, the simplest tactic is to loose-feed maggots or casters, keeping a steady trickle going in. Perch can also respond to chopped worm introduced using a bait dropper. For bream and skimmers try groundbait to kickstart the swim and loose-fed maggots and casters over the top of the bed of bait.

Rigs for this type of canal are similar to those that are suitable for deep stillwaters. A float taking 1g with a fine bristle is adequate for 10ft of water, perhaps increased to 1.25 or 1.5g if the water is much deeper. Concentrate nearly all of the weight in a bulk around 3ft from the hook, with just No. 11 shot droppers spaced out below this. Rig these on 0.12mm line with hook links of 0.08 or 0.09mm and fine-wire hooks to match. There is certainly a degree of finesse needed on this type of water. If you are targeting bigger bream and perch, you will need to step up the gear accordingly.

There will often be a slight draw on this type of canal so use the pole to steady the presentation of the bait and ease the rig through the swim.

Drains

Tackle drains in much the same way as you would other similar waters – some resemble barge canals, others are more like ship canals. One difference from canals is that, on some drains, the banks are much steeper, at the base of flood banks or even close to roads. This can make shipping back tricky at best, and hazardous at worst. Drains often have a good head of bream and tench, and a more positive approach for these can pay dividends. Chopped worm is particularly effective for tench, and feeding plenty of casters can hold a bream shoal.

11 BUILD ON YOUR KNOWLEDGE

Fishing with a pole is an addictive method and can be deadly, and you can transfer some of the pole-fishing methods to conventional rod-and-reel fishing. For example, there is no reason why you should not use a pole float for margin fishing, or even river trotting.

There are many more possible permutations of tackle, rig, bait and feeding pattern than this book can cover, and new methods are continually evolving. (Indeed, many methods have been specifically conceived for pole fishing, evolved over the decades, become popular, and then faded away. One good example is eel fishing on the Fenland rivers, which was vital in the late 1980s and early 90s, but became obsolete when the eels vanished.)

Despite the new tackle, technology, baits and methods, however, the basics of pole fishing remain constant. This book should have laid the foundations for you, by providing the essential knowledge upon which inexperienced and improving anglers can develop their pole fishing skills. More experienced pole anglers will always benefit from thinking more deeply about their pole fishing, expanding their knowledge and learning new ways in which they can catch fish with a pole.

There are no magic methods, baits or items of tackle in any type of fishing. Simplicity is the key to success, and yet in pole fishing there are a multitude of little factors that make all the difference. There are also many myths, repeated time and time again, which you would do well to ignore!

The key factors that lead to angling success are always worth repeating:

- Locate the fish.
- Avoid scaring the fish.

- Fish at the right time.
- Choose the right tackle; and
- Choose the right bait.

The last two are the most pertinent to the pole angler, since they represent the areas in which the pole angler can genuinely gain an advantage over those using the more conventional rod and reel. In the right hands, bait presentation using a pole is unsurpassed, and there is little doubt that, when it comes to detecting bites, the pole angler is in a class of his own.

That does not mean that the pole angler can neglect the first three factors of success, any more than other anglers can.

There are few rules when fishing the pole: providing you plumb accurately and feed precisely, and ensure a delicate and precise bait presentation, you should not go far wrong. Practice is vital to get the best out of pole fishing and it helps enormously if a good pole angler can show you the ropes. If possible, each time you pole fish, try a different swim, a different float, a different way of fishing. Try different baits and experiment with feeding patterns. Learn to feed more than one area of the swim, beginning with a close-in line and a spot further out. Ensure that you plumb both spots carefully, and maintain the feeding for both spots.

See if you can be selective in what you are catching, and learn how a swim develops over the course of a session. Consider what is happening if you regularly get a pattern of a slow start for half an hour, then a short flurry of activity, followed by very little. This is a common pattern for novices but with practice you will learn to develop swims that get stronger and stronger. It is all about regular feeding rather

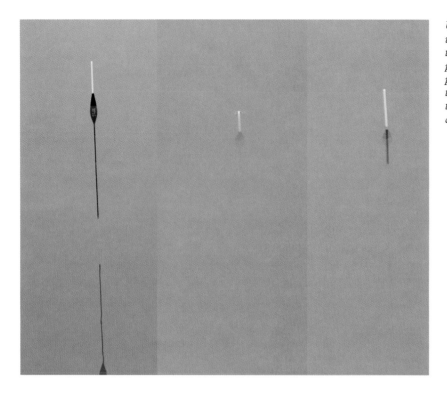

Understanding the underwater contours through careful plumbing is vital to pole-fishing success: too deep (far left), too shallow (centre), and just right (left).

than erratic feeding. Once you feel comfortable with feeding two areas, try feeding three areas.

Remember that fishing with a short pole rather than a long one can offer many advantages, always allowing that you can catch the fish closer in. It is easier to see bites, fish more sensitively, feed more accurately, fish with less effort and, in match conditions, simply catch fish much faster.

Good preparation will contribute to your success in pole fishing. This includes making up rigs and tying hooks at home, but it can extend much further. Get to know your chosen venues by spending time watching and talking to other anglers (taking care not to disturb their fishing). Spend time preparing your baits and keep bait boxes clean, remembering that good bait means good bites. Look after your pole and the fitted elastics; replace elastics frequently, and wipe down poles, especially the joints, to keep them clean of dirt. Check floats for cracks that could cause them to leak or fall apart. Ensure you have spare line, shot and hooks for rig making,

and do not forget to take all your gadgets with you. Dry your nets after each session and check them for damage. Clear out the rubbish from your box and bait carrier each time you get home; this is far better than finding mouldy sandwiches next time out, or wondering what that strange smell is.

Is watercraft dead when it comes to pole fishing modern man-made waters? Or is pole fishing pure technique? Far from it. On these venues you still need to find the fish without scaring them. You need to understand what is happening underwater, and then plan how to feed the swim and present your hook bait. The difference in catches on commercial fisheries between novices and top-class anglers is significant, and yet the top anglers use surprisingly simple methods. Their feeding is accurate, measured and regular; their bait presentation is spot on and adapted to how the fish are responding. They are not afraid to experiment, always looking for an edge, and they understand the prevailing water conditions.

There is no guarantee that you will always catch fish when pole fishing.

Ideal pole fishing: a warm day, plenty of fish and time to relax.

Match-fishing legend Ivan Marks often explained the importance of trying to think like a fish. He asked himself what he would expect if he were the fish. He did get some of the answers. He learnt how bream shoals behaved, and put it to devastating use on waters such as the Welland, Witham and Great Ouse Relief Channel, persuading the bream shoals to settle in his swim through crafty groundbaiting. He found out how to catch big roach on those same rivers in tough match conditions, understanding the very different feeding and bait presentation needed, and the necessity of good bait. Underpinning his success was a humble approach to finding out what the fish wanted rather than using his tactics to dictate to the fish.

Simplicity is that divine art of removing the clutter and the unnecessary from what you do.

Many anglers persist in over-complicating things, seeing problems where none exist, and confusing themselves. If only they could discover the magic gadget, or bait or method that will unlock the doors to success, then their results would surely outshine those of the stars. Yet all the while a simpler approach would make a huge difference.

Pole fishing is a fun method, as pleasurable or frustrating as any other when things go well or badly, as the case may be. This book should lead you to increased angling success, and plenty of enjoyment along the way.

All the best,
Mark Wintle
Graham Marsden

FURTHER READING
& INFORMATION

Books

Over the past thirty years there have been a number of books on pole and general match fishing. Many seem dated now, mainly owing to the rapid growth in commercial fisheries, but all offer some insight into pole fishing. Almost all of the following are out of print but worth finding, usually at modest prices via second-hand bookshops or eBay.

Ashurst, Kevin, *World Class Match Fishing*, Cassell, 1977.

Ashurst, Kevin, *The Encyclopaedia of Pole Fishing*, Pelham, 1983.

Dennis, Paul, *An Introduction to Match Fishing*, Crowood, 1992.

Dennis, Paul, *Match Fishing – The Winner's Peg*, Crowood, 1989.

Haines, Allan, *The Complete Book of Match Fishing*, David & Charles, 1992.

Haines, Allan, *The Complete Book of Float Fishing*, David & Charles, 1989.

Legge, Tom, *The Fox Match Guide to Commercial Fisheries*, Fox Match, 2006.

Milsom, Kim, *Match Fishing*, Crowood, 1994.

Nudd, Bob, *How to Be the World's Best Fisherman*, Boxtree, 1993.

Nudd, Bob, *Bob Nudd's Illustrated Guide to Pole Fishing*, EMAP Active, 1998.

Pickering, Tom, *My Way with the Pole*, Pisces, 1989.

Swinscoe, Wayne and Slaymaker, Don, *Pole Fishing*, Beekay, 1990.

Wilson, John, *Coarse Fishing Method Book*, Boxtree, 1997.

Magazines

Magazines specializing in match fishing are few but monthly magazines *Match Fishing* and *Advanced Pole Fishing* both have plenty for the pole angler. Weekly newspapers *Angling Times* and *Angler's Mail* also have some how-to-do-it pole fishing features.

Websites

The following sites may be of interest, with general articles as well as information on waters, bait and tackle:

fishingmagic.com
woodlandviewfishery.co.uk
todbermanor.co.uk
daiwasports.co.uk
foxint.com
garbolino.fr
maver.co.uk
prestoninnovations.com
sensas.fr
shakespeare-fishing.co.uk
shimano.com
sonubaits.co.uk
trabucco.it
vandeneyndebaits.com
zebco-europe.com (Browning)

INDEX